The NORFOLK Cook Book

with Norfolk Food & Drink

A celebration of the amazing food & drink on our doorstep.
Featuring over 50 stunning recipes.

The Norfolk Cook Book

©2017 Meze Publishing. All rights reserved.

First edition printed in 2017 in the UK.

ISBN: 978-1-910863-23-7

*Thank you to: Galton Blackiston, Morston Hall
Richard Bainbridge, Benedicts
Anna Stevenson, Norfolk Food & Drink*

Compiled by: Lisa Pullen

Written by: Aaron Jackson, Kate Reeves-Brown,
Kerre Chen

Photography by: Tim Green
(www.timgreenphotographer.co.uk)

Edited by: Phil Turner

Designed by: Matt Crowder, Paul Cocker,
Jake Cowlishaw

PR: Kerre Chen

Cover art: Luke Prest (www.lukeprest.com)

Contributors: Sarah Koriba, Imogen Green

me:ze
PUBLISHING

Published by Meze Publishing Limited

Unit 1b Rialto

2 Kelham Square

Kelham Riverside

Sheffield S3 8SD

Web: www.mezepublishing.co.uk

Tel: 0114 275 7709

Email: info@mezepublishing.co.uk

Printed by Bell & Bain Ltd, Glasgow

FOREWORD

Proud holder of a Michelin-star since 1998, Galton Blackiston is the Norfolk food scene's most famous son. He recently celebrated 25 years at Morston Hall while his latest venture, No.1 Cromer has proved a resounding success. Here, he shares his thoughts on what makes his home county so special.

Well how do I begin to sum up in a few words what Norfolk means to me?

I was born and brought up here many moons ago, back in the days when holidays were rarely taken abroad, but instead by the British seaside; hence my deep affection for our wonderful Norfolk coastline.

Like many of us Norfolk folk, the lure of returning home having spent time away learning my trade was very strong. Once that dream was realised 25 years ago, my wife Tracy and I set about creating a little gem on the North Norfolk coast, Morston Hall. Our principles were simple back in those days, and they remain so now. We use very seasonal produce to create exciting yet achievable dishes. I'm biased I know, but in my eyes, there is no finer area to live and run a business or two. And although the words seasonality and provenance might be trendy and hip at the moment, they have always played a huge part in the planning and success of Morston Hall. It makes sense to use vegetables and fruits when in season and 18 years of a Michelin star is surely testament to that. We have a wonderful plethora of seasonal produce in our back yard and it is a real pleasure being able to showcase just what this county has to offer; whether it be asparagus in May, samphire in July or Brussels sprouts in the winter. You name it; we've got it all in this wonderful county of ours.

The real beauty of Norfolk is the fact that as time passes, not a lot changes. We still have no motorway within the county and although life is very busy on the coast there remains a real sense of ruralness, which is something I have always treasured.

Having spent the last 25 years running a business in Morston and in the last four an incredible fish and chip business in Cromer, I do feel qualified in being able to eulogise about 'my' Norfolk. I'm sure everyone who buys the Norfolk Cook Book will enjoy the wonderful recipes within, and above all, get a real sense of what makes the county's cooking so special.

Galton Blackiston

Chef proprietor at Morston Hall

FOREWORD

Richard Bainbridge is one of the talented chefs putting Norfolk on the culinary map, by showcasing the amazing produce available in this beautiful county at his restaurant Benedicts. Here, he shares what makes Norfolk such a special place to be a chef.

Norfolk is my home and I am so proud of it, but it was a place I could not wait to leave the first chance I had when I was young. I travelled the world and the seven seas, seeing all the wonders and everything on offer. However, Norfolk was always on my mind and in my heart, so the return home was somewhat inevitable for me.

Coming home was a chance to show Katja my wife what an amazing place Norfolk is, from the famous high skies to the beautiful coast line, not to mention its famous sunset, which is a thing of true beauty. There are countless other wonders that are unique to Norfolk, but the one thing that makes it the best place on earth has to be the people in it. From their sense of humour to their love for everything Norfolk… especially its food.

There is so much to be proud of when it comes to Norfolk's food. From the world-class barley that is transported around the globe to the hard-working farmers who work the land to produce some of the best produce this country has to offer. The potatoes, shallots and rapeseed, for example, are incredible. To the smallholders who care for the livestock that makes its way to my kitchen at Benedicts and to the Norfolk fishermen, for without them, the stories of the Cromer crab, Brancaster mussel and the rest of the amazing seafood that lives along our shores would remain unknown and untold.

Finally, on to the small and tiny businesses that work tirelessly to showcase our county for the world to see – amazing cheese-makers, producers of cured meats and millers to name a few. I have a saying about the plethora of produce that comes from our little county, which I sum up simply as the "bounty of the county".

Richard Bainbridge

Chef proprietor at Benedicts

CONTENTS

Welcome to NORFOLK

Norfolk is not only a wonderful place to live, but a favourite destination for holiday-makers who choose Norfolk Country Cottages as a place to enjoy the stunning landscape.

"With agriculture at its heart, and a 93-mile coastline to boot, it's not surprising that Norfolk's food offering is so rich and varied," says Lucy Downing of Norfolk Country Cottages. The coastline is hugely important to the county and it shapes much of the menus of the region. The seas provide everything from Brancaster mussels and oysters to the sweetest Cromer crabs that live on the recently discovered chalk ridge.

The weather, too, makes Norfolk a special place. "One of the driest and sunniest climates in the country, this provides ideal growing conditions for malting barley. Cue the UK's greatest concentration of micro-breweries," Lucy explains.

The grand estates and rich countryside nurture a decadent variety of game, which all appear on the menus of restaurants throughout the region, whilst the farmers supply Norfolk's growing number of specialist butchers and farm shops.

In recent years, this infatuation with food has given dawn to a whole new foodie scene, ripe with unique and experimental producers making everything from saffron liqueurs and venison bresaola to award-winning goat cheeses and chocolate granola.

"As a local company, we have always been passionate about Norfolk," Lucy continues. "Not only do we support Norfolk Food & Drink, but we also continuously strive to encourage the visitors we bring to the county to taste, sip and explore our wonderful culinary fare. No matter whether they choose to meander around one of our excellent farmers' markets and cook back at their cottage, or relax in one of Norfolk's fabulous restaurants or pubs, they are guaranteed a flavourful holiday to remember… and usually re-visit for a second helping too!"

Photo: Tim Green

Photography: Steve Flanagan/the Original Cottage Company

Celebrating food and drink
IN NORFOLK

Established in 2004, Norfolk Food & Drink is a not-for-profit organisation which has been dedicated to celebrating the burgeoning food and drink industry in Norfolk for 12 years.

Norfolk Food & Drink is the 'go to' organisation for all things related to food and drink in the county, but what do they actually do?

First and foremost, they encourage everybody to have a better understanding of the importance of food and drink to Norfolk's economy, environment, health and well-being, countryside and agriculture.

Norfolk Food & Drink plays an important role in encouraging visitors to Norfolk, as well as generating a community spirit across the county. Residents participate in the many Food & Drink events taking place throughout the year, creating a food community that incorporates people from every part of the industry.

They offer free marketing, PR and business support to food and drink retailers, producers, restaurants and bars across the county. As this is an area many smaller businesses lack the time, experience or resources to fulfil, this is a helpful resource for busy producers and restaurateurs who are concentrating on developing their businesses.

Working in partnership with sponsors, local businesses and organisations, Norfolk Food & Drink promotes and supports the food and drink industry in Norfolk. It is a team effort that involves a plethora of local organisations, such as the Norwich BID, county councils, Visit Norfolk and Visit Norwich, as well as the local media including Radio Norfolk, Future Radio and their award-winning media partner, Archant. Working together with all of these partners, they celebrate the food and drink industry in Norfolk.

"As a not-for-profit organisation, our success is down to the amazing support we receive from volunteers and sponsors. So, we would like to say a huge THANK YOU to all those companies who invest their time and money into making Norfolk Food & Drink what it is today, and helping us to applaud and salute food and drink in Norfolk. Thank you all!" - Norfolk Food & Drink.

You can find out more about Norfolk Food & Drink and the mouth-watering events they promote, by visiting www.norfolkfoodanddrink.com.

Photo: Steve Flanagan/The
Original Cottage Company

Norfolk Food & Drink
PATRONS

Norfolk Food & Drink is honoured to have four of the county's best-loved and best-known chefs and restaurateurs as patrons, supporting the work they do.

Nick Mills

After working in some of London's finest hotels and restaurants, including the Royal Court Hotel, Sloane Square, The Capital Hotel and La Gavroche, Nick first joined Brasted's as a part-time waiter in 1991, whilst studying a BSc in Business Management at UEA and a BA in Hospitality at Norwich City College. In 1994, Nick was made General Manager, and in 2000, Managing Director. He has always had a huge passion for food, wine and all things 'industry'. This, coupled with his position at Brasted's, has enabled him to champion Norfolk and its many and varied high-quality food and drink producers. Nick has been an integral member of the steering committee of Norfolk Food & Drink since it was founded in 2004.

Vanessa Scott

Vanessa Scott and her husband Les set up the boutique hotel Strattons in the market town of Swaffham in 1990. The site now also includes a café/deli and Vanessa has won considerable plaudits for both quality and her policy of sustainably sourcing local ingredients. Strattons became the first hotel in the UK to win the Queen's Award for Outstanding Environmental Performance and Green Globe's Best Small Global Hotel, and was the first restaurant in the UK to receive the RSPCA Ethical Food award. Vanessa has been named EDP Food & Drink Hero and Outstanding Achievement winner. In 2011, she spearheaded the first Brecks Food Festival, which won an Action for Market Towns award. She is a regular culinary contributor to Radio Norfolk's Garden Party.

Richard Hughes

Beginning his career in the kitchen as a 15-year-old at The Imperial Hotel in Great Yarmouth, Richard opened his first restaurant – Number 24 in Wymondham – in 1991. During his 11 years in Wymondham, he also taught at the Hotel School at Norwich City College and began his popular Step by Step column in EDP Norfolk Magazine. In 2002, he left Wymondham to open The Lavender House at Brundall, and very shortly after founded the Richard Hughes Cookery School. Winning the inaugural British Cookery School of the year, 2017 saw him relocate the school to the Grade I-listed heritage site that is The Assembly House in the centre of Norwich, where Richard is Chef Director.

Chris Coubrough

New Zealander Chris Coubrough worked at top restaurants in Switzerland, London and Suffolk before settling on the 'Saltmarsh Coast' more than 14 years ago. His upbringing on a remote farm on New Zealand's North Island nurtured a love of food and the outdoor life which have driven him to hone his cookery skills to perfection. Dad-of-two Chris is the owner of The Crown Hotel in Wells-next-the-Sea and The Ship Hotel in Brancaster. In 2014 Chris, who previously hosted ITV Anglia's Coastal Kitchen cookery series, received the Outstanding Achievement Award at the EDP Food & Drink Awards. The judges made special mention of the role he had played in helping to establish the North Norfolk Food & Drink Festival as one of the county's biggest annual events.

The Norwich Food & Drink FESTIVAL

As well as promoting the many and varied food and drink events which take place across Norfolk throughout the year, Norfolk Food & Drink is proud to host its own flagship event – The Norwich Food & Drink Festival.

Now in its 13th year, The Norwich Food & Drink Festival is a celebration of Norfolk's food and drink industry, right in the heart of historic Norwich.

The festival is traditionally held on Father's Day, in and around one of the city's most iconic buildings – The Forum – and also sees the closure of a number of roads, as it accommodates a huge variety of food and drink producers, butchers, retailers, chefs and entertainers, all offering a host of exciting food and drink related offerings for families to enjoy.

Sponsored by one of the city's most prestigious law firms, Cozens-Hardy solicitors, the Norwich Food & Drink Festival attracts visitors from across Norfolk and beyond as it offers a stunning programme of events with plenty for all the family to enjoy.

The Adnams Beer Garden is a particular highlight, along with the Producers' Street Market which is packed with delicious local food and drink to buy. There is also a Cookery Demonstration Theatre featuring some of the county's best-loved and best-known chefs. For the children, there is the Kids Zone, which is sure to keep them entertained. With live music happening too, the atmosphere is something special.

In addition, the now legendary Battle of the Bangers, also takes place at the foot of the City Hall. This famous competition gives the public the opportunity to sample ten of the county's best sausages and vote for their favourite, as the butchers battle it out to win the judges' blind taste award as well as the public vote.

The Norwich Food & Drink Festival is a place to see, smell and taste the amazing food of Norfolk all in one place.

Proudly NORFOLK

The Proudly Norfolk initiative is helping people in the Norfolk Food & Drink industry to champion the county's amazing produce and dining scene.

An initiative which was established by Norfolk Food & Drink to champion the county's delicious food and drink has evolved into a membership scheme for producers, restaurateurs, café owners and retailers to spread the word about the bounty of the county.

Proudly Norfolk Food & Drink is an accredited business-to-business membership scheme for Norfolk businesses in the food and drink industry, which brings them together in their common purpose of highlighting their commitment to promoting food and drink in Norfolk.

Membership is open to anyone in the industry and, once qualified, members can enjoy a range of benefits designed to emphasise their integrity and passion for local produce, and to give credence to their business.

For consumers, Proudly Norfolk Food & Drink is a brand they can trust and a mark of quality, ensuring the producer from whom they are buying or the restaurant in which they are eating cares passionately about the quality and integrity of the food and drink they are producing.

"As a Proudly Norfolk producer, I think the Proudly Norfolk membership scheme is a great way to give our customers confidence in our products," says Candi Robertson of Candi's Chutney.

Becoming a member costs just £25.00 + VAT per annum, and the range of benefits is certainly long and diverse.

These benefits include a directory listing on the Norfolk Food & Drink website, with a link back to the business's own site, as well as the opportunity to be included in the Proudly Norfolk news section in the Norfolk Food & Drink monthly newsletter. As this newsletter goes to over 5000 people, it is a great way to have a local company seen by lots of people in the area. Helping local producers and businesses to be visible to customers in Norfolk is one of the most important aspects of the Proudly Norfolk scheme. That is why members are also given a window sticker, which can be used to display in a premises or car, and a certificate, which can be proudly displayed for customers to see.

As well as those physical marketing tools, there is also a digital marketing support pack for members too. This includes the Proudly logo, which members can use on their own marketing materials, for example menus, packaging, marketing materials, website, social media and e-signatures. There are also lots of ideas on how to make the most out of membership.

All members are invited to attend two exclusive members networking events per annum, which are ideal opportunities to meet other local producers, makers and restaurateurs in the local area.

As Norfolk Food & Drink continues to grow and develop, there are certainly going to be myriad other initiatives and opportunities that occur as part of the Proudly Norfolk membership scheme.

Being part of the Proudly Norfolk scheme is something that members want to celebrate and shout about as much as possible. Mini labels with the Proudly Norfolk Food & Drink logo on are available to buy – perfect for adding to packaging!

The most important part of being a member is perhaps simply being part of an innovative and inspiring foodie community. Being introduced to other fellow Proudly Norfolk members helps everybody to make the most of the incredible food and drink community of the county.

Norfolk Food & Drink

THE NELSON

Charlie Hodson's award-winning sausage roll... with love from Norfolk. Raised and educated in Norfolk, Charlie Hodson is a real ambassador for the food, drink and farming industry in Norfolk. A chef and entrepreneur, Charlie owns Charlie's Norfolk Food Heroes, which champions the local food and drink industry. Charlie is also a patron of the Porkstock festival, a regional ambassador for Marie Curie UK, RNLI crew at Cromer, chef consultant for The Globe at Wells and supporter of the YANA project.

Preparation time: 30 minutes | Cooking time: 20-30 minutes | Serves 6

Ingredients

Couple of strands of Norfolk saffron

1 tsp Crush cold-pressed rapeseed oil

650g sausage meat from Tim Allens Pork Norfolk (available from Archers Norwich, Icarus Hines Cromer, Walsingham Farm Shop)

285g Fruit Pig Company fresh blood black pudding, broken down into 1cm pieces

15ml Wildknight East Anglian vodka

2 tbsp Candi's carrot chutney

Pinch of Maldon sea salt

Pinch of black pepper

500g puff pastry

Flour, for dusting

1 Wayland egg, beaten

Method

Preheat the oven to 180°c (fan). Crush the saffron using a pestle and mortar and add the rapeseed oil. In a large bowl combine the sausage meat, black pudding, vodka, chutney, salt, pepper and saffron/oil mixture. Mix by hand. Don't be tempted to use a mixer as it will break the mixture down too finely, simply bind it together.

Roll out the puff pastry to 3mm thickness into a rectangular shape, flouring both sides as you roll.

Place two rolls of sausage meat mix (with 10cm between each roll) horizontally across the sheet of pastry.

Egg wash the pastry and fold it from top to middle, and cut. Repeat the process on the other line of sausage meat. Crimp the pastry edges (I simply use a fork or knife point).

Cut into six and place on a non-stick baking tray or parchment-lined baking tray. (to keep your knives at their best, don't be tempted to cut whilst on the metal tray).

Egg wash the outer pastry and ends. Bake in the preheated oven for approximately 20-30 minutes. Cool a little and serve with my very own sauce, Charlie's Food Heroes BBQ Sauce.

RASPBERRY ROSE CHOCOLATE MERINGUE PIE

Kate Barmby is a home cook, mum, nurse, farmer's daughter, community volunteer, columnist and contestant on the Great British Bake Off 2016. She grew up on her parents' farm in South Norfolk, close to where she now lives with her own family. As a contestant on the Great British Bake Off, she championed the fantastic produce Norfolk has on offer including local meat, oils, cheeses, flour and fruits by taking them with her and including them in her recipes.

Preparation time: 15 minutes | Cooking time: 40 minutes | Serves 4

Ingredients

For the sweet chocolate pastry:

175g Golden Jewel pastry flour, plus extra for dusting

50g cocoa powder

Pinch of salt

150g icing sugar

150g unsalted butter, chilled and cubed

3 large free-range egg yolks

1 whole free-range egg, lightly beaten, for glazing

For the raspberry filling:

500g fresh raspberries

60g cornflour

75g caster sugar

100ml cold water

2 lemons, juiced (reserve 1 tsp for meringue)

3 large free-range egg yolks

60g unsalted butter

For the meringue:

4 large free-range egg whites

Pinch of salt

1 tsp lemon juice

225g Essence Foods Norfolk rose caster sugar, petals sifted out and reserved for decoration (alternatively regular caster sugar and ¼ tsp rose water)

Method

For the sweet chocolate pastry

Process the dry ingredients in a food processor until evenly mixed. Add the butter. Pulse until the butter has been incorporated. Lightly beat the egg yolks and gradually add to the mixture whilst pulsing until it is barely combined. You may not need all of the egg yolks. Tip the mix out onto the work surface and gently bring it together with your hands. Wrap in cling film and chill for 20 minutes. Roll the pastry out to 5mm thickness between two sheets of flour-dusted baking parchment. Preheat the oven to 170°c (fan) and put a baking sheet on the top shelf.

Lightly grease the tin, then carefully transfer the pastry to line the tin, overlapping the top of the tin. Prick the base all over with a fork. Put in the freezer for 5–10 minutes to firm up.

Line the pastry case with lightly greased baking parchment and fill completely with baking beans. Bake for 25 minutes on the hot baking sheet. Carefully remove the baking beans and baking parchment. Trim off any excess pastry with a serrated knife and brush the bottom of the pastry case with lightly beaten egg. Return to the oven and cook for a further 5–10 minutes.

For the raspberry filling

Blitz the raspberries and push the pulp through a fine metal sieve to remove the seeds. You should end up with about 350ml purée. Put the cornflour and caster sugar into a large jug and mix with a little of the water to make a paste. Add the remaining water and the lemon juice to the purée. Bring this up to the boil and then tip over the cornflour paste, stirring vigorously until smooth. Pour into a saucepan and heat gently, stirring until thick and glossy. Take the pan off the heat and beat in the egg yolks and then the butter. Allow to cool slightly before pouring it into the pastry case.

For the meringue

Reduce the oven to 130°c (fan). Put the egg whites into the bowl of a stand mixer fitted with a whisk attachment and beat on medium speed, then add the salt and lemon juice and keep whisking the egg whites until they are stiff but not dry. Slowly pour the caster sugar into the egg whites with the mixer still running. Scrape down any stray sugar from the sides of the bowl and keep whisking until the meringue is stiff and glossy.

Scrape the meringue into a very large disposable piping bag fitted with a 2cm closed star nozzle. Pipe roses on top of the pie to create a bouquet effect. Transfer the pie still on the baking sheet to the oven and bake for 30-40 minutes until the surface feels crisp and dry but there is still the promise of marshmallowy softness underneath. Leave to cool for at least 20 minutes before removing the tin.

Inspiring PASSION

One thing that unites all those working in the hospitality industry is the extraordinary passion for ingredients, cooking, service and quality, which is something that A Passion to Inspire has been nurturing in young people since 2009.

Initially developed to create stronger links between education and industry, A Passion to Inspire is a charity that works with colleges, farms and top chefs to inspire, encourage and support students in their chosen careers.

From its initial format as a competition, the non-profit-making initiative was founded by Murray Chapman in 2009 and has expanded to work with over 160 colleges, including City College Norwich, College of West Anglia, West Suffolk College, Cambridge Regional College and Colchester Institute. It is open to all students at any level, including front of house and kitchen.

From visits to RSPCA Assured-approved farms, Nurtured in Norfolk, Anglia Free-range Eggs, Norfolk Quail and Great farms like Dingley Dell Pork, to taking part in the Flying Visit programme, it gives students the chance to be involved in major industry events, get to meet top chefs, restaurateurs and hoteliers, as well as producers, growers and suppliers. Through their charity dinners, A Passion to Inspire has raised over a staggering £150,000 for charities such as NSPCC, Teenage Cancer Trust and Hospitality Action.

It's not only the students who get to enjoy being part of this dynamic initiative, the incredible list of chefs who work with them also relish being involved with the innovative project. Richard Bainbridge, Charlie Hodson, Chris 'Buzz' Busby, Richard Goldings, Roger Hickman, Nick Mills and Eric Snaith are just a handful of local chefs who have worked with A Passion to Inspire.

"I have been involved with A Passion to Inspire from the start. The charity works with over 160 colleges and hundreds of students, inspiring them to create great food and, more importantly, develop themselves in our fantastic industry," says Mark Poynton, Chef Patron at Michelin-star Alimentum Restaurant, which also boasts 3 AA rosettes.

"Everyone knows that involving young aspiring student chefs in any kitchen will always lead to them achieving success and a definite strong platform for high achievement in the future. To work with young enthusiastic and talented students and chefs is always an honour, spreading the knowledge to them on new cultures and foods from different continents is a pleasure. At Passion much is done to Inspire young people to hit above and beyond their small goals and ambitions, which makes it a magnificent organisation that aims to help in achieving these goals!! For me it is a joy to work with them and help them help young people on their journey of success." Says Cyrus Todiwala OBE DL DBA of Café Spice Namaste.

With the involvement of people from the entire industry – from farm to front of house – A Passion to Inspire helps and supports the future of tomorrow today.

City College Norwich

ENGLISH LEMON CUSTARD PUDDING, POPPY AND SESAME SEED SNAP WITH RASPBERRY COULIS

Chef lecturer at City College Norwich, Bob Oberhoffer, has proven how successful you can become with a hospitality and catering qualification. With a career spanning over 30 years, Bob has worked his way up from an apprentice chef in the British Army to owning a two AA rosette restaurant. "The hospitality and catering industry is full of opportunities for those with excellent people skills and the right attitude. Becoming successful in the sector requires lots of determination and self-discipline as well as a strong work ethic. However, the skills that are learnt along the way can be applied to any job and will see those who are willing to work hard quickly progress to senior management roles.

Working with A Passion to Inspire is an incredibly exciting opportunity for students to develop their experience of work, broaden their horizons and refine their higher technical skills in real time. Working with these industry leaders will give them an excellent opportunity to develop working relationships and future employment." he says.

Preparation time: 15 minutes | Cooking time: 40 minutes | Serves 4

Ingredients

For the custard pudding:

2 lemons, zest and juice

85g caster sugar

3 eggs

250ml double cream

Pinch of cinnamon

For the raspberry coulis:

250g frozen raspberries

50g icing sugar

60g liquid glucose

For the poppy and sesame seed snap:

50g unsalted butter

50g sugar

20g glucose

20g milk

100g sesame seeds

20g poppy seeds

To serve:

8 raspberries

8 blueberries

8 small strawberries (small)

Method

For the custard pudding

Combine the lemon juice and sugar in a pan, and heat to make a syrup. Pour the lemon syrup over the eggs in a bowl and whisk. Bring the cream to the boil in a separate pan, then whisk into the egg and lemon mixture, along with the cinnamon. Pass the mixture through a fine sieve onto the lemon zest in a heatproof bowl. Slowly cook over a bain-marie (water bath) for 15-20 minutes, then divide into four ramekins and chill.

For the raspberry coulis

Cover the frozen raspberries with icing sugar and allow to defrost at room temperature. Pass the raspberries through a medium sieve then through muslin. Add the glucose to correct the consistency of the coulis.

For the poppy and sesame seed snaps

Preheat the oven to 200°c. Combine all the ingredients in a saucepan except the seeds. Heat on the stove to dissolve the sugar, then bring to the boil and add the seeds. Put the mixture onto a silicon mat or silicon paper-lined baking sheet and bake in the preheated oven until golden brown. Cut and shape the biscuits as desired.

To serve

Coat the fruit with raspberry coulis. Sprinkle the puddings with caster sugar and caramelise the tops with a blowtorch. Serve the puddings with the coulis-coated fruit and the poppy and sesame seed snaps.

A Family AFFAIR

Family-run Norwich landmark takes aim...

If we are what we eat, then it stands to reason that we should only eat the best. Luckily for the inhabitants of Norwich, and those venturing from further afield, Archer's provides exactly that.

Archer's began life in 1929, when John Archer opened the shop on Plumstead Road that the business still operates from today. The butchery is award-winning, regularly coming out on top in 'battles of the bangers' for its sausages and prime cuts. Archer's doesn't just stop at sourcing its pork, beef, and lamb from local farms. The meat is free-range whenever possible, with feed ratios, seasonality, and even specific breeds selected to ensure the finest flavours all-year round.

It isn't just Sunday roast staples, though. Cuts that regularly used to appear on tables throughout the land are all available, alongside impeccably-sourced poultry, game, and venison, and enough flavoursome stock, dripping, and marrowbones to gladden the hearts of the traditionalist, gourmand, and those searching for something a little different.

Archer's is more than just a carnivore's delight, though. Launched by John's son, Jimmy, the delicatessen offers a full selection of home-cooked cold cuts, freshly-prepared seasonal salads and Antipasti, as well as traditional homemade products such as pork-and-onion dripping, potted meats, and pies and pastries.

In fact, for those who love the idea of home-cooked food but who don't want to go to the hassle of cooking it themselves, Archer's provides cooking, delivery, and takeaway services! If you're after something special, they produce a range of home-style, freshly-prepared meals such as moussaka and beef bourguinon. For those who want to take their barbecue skills one step further, Archer's provides bespoke BBQ hampers bulging with high-class burgers, sausages, ribs, wings and marinades. There is even a full hog roast kit – perfect for large parties on long summer evenings.

On top of that, Archer's baguette takeaway service isn't just a welcome addition for the leg-weary tourist and the lunchtime office worker. It's become part of the local vocabulary, with those heading to Carrow Road for kickoff stopping in 'for an Archers' on their way to the match.

If this seems like a dizzying amount of choice, well, it's all very simple – it's about all about great food.

"Everything has grown organically from the first principles my grandfather established," explains Jamie, the third generation Archer to own and run the business. "Supplying the best quality to his customers was what he did and it remains at the heart of what we do today."

Quality first, price second – an ethos that serves Archer's and its customers as well today as it did when John Archer first launched the business ...

ARCHER'S

HIGH CLASS
FAMILY BUTCHERS
SINCE 19

Fax 01603 434305

Archer's Butchers
ITALIAN SAUSAGE LINGUINI

We might love the best of British here at Archer's Butchers, but we're also huge fans of the way our Italian cousins use food: take the best basic high-quality ingredients and combine them to create a dish that bursts with flavour and character. Featuring our 'Great Taste' award-winning Italian sausages, this is such a simple recipe, but its hearty and flavoursome and can be served up at any time of year for the whole family or groups of friends.

Preparation time: 5 minutes | Cooking time: 30 minutes | Serves 4

Ingredients

500g or 6 x large Italian sausages

Crush Foods rapeseed oil

450g good quality dried or homemade linguini

6 shallots, diced

One handful of Norfolk cherry tomatoes (when in season)

150ml white wine

1 squirt of lemon juice

300ml crème fraîche

Handful of flat leaf parsley, chopped

Grated Parmesan cheese

Cracked black pepper

Maldon Sea salt

Method

Gently fry off the sausages in a large frying pan with a little rapeseed oil until golden brown in colour and cooked all the way through. Midway through cooking, place a lid on the pan to retain some of the juice.

While the sausages are cooking, add the linguini to a boiling pan of salt water and leave to cook for approximately 10 minutes.

Once cooked, remove the sausages from the pan, chop into smaller pieces, and then set aside.

Soften the shallots in the juice and fat from the sausages. Then add the tomatoes and fry for only a couple of minutes. Do not overcook them otherwise they will turn to mush and lose their sweetness.

Deglaze the pan with the wine and lemon juice and reduce the liquid by half.

Add the sausage pieces, warm through for approximately one minute and then mix in the crème fraîche. Add salt and pepper to taste.

Draining the cooked linguini, add it to the pan and mix thoroughly.

Finish with chopped parsley and Parmesan cheese.

Serve up with a fresh loaf of crusty bread, a large glass of white wine, and good company!

From farmyard to FOOD HALL

Back to the garden began back in 2002 when Lord and Lady Hastings converted 1000 acres of farmland to organic production and decided to set up a vegetable stall throughout the following summer.

By the Easter of 2004, they had moved the operation into the barn. The roof leaked and the previous occupants had been a herd of cows, but at least it was mostly dry and it was out of the wind. After a big renovation in 2007, Back to the garden was transformed into the stunning food hall that it is today, which includes a café, butchery, delicatessen and a tranquil garden. The magnificent scale of its construction, its soaring oak-beamed roof, and its enchanting garden means that it lends itself perfectly to wedding parties and celebrations.

From the start, the aim was to produce food that was traceable, local and had a 'just-picked' freshness to it. A place that celebrated the small-scale and personal. They have always aimed to bring together people who are as enthusiastic about fresh produce as themselves, many of their clientele have been coming from the start and for good reason too.

There is a passion and commitment that go into sourcing and producing food, which distinguishes Back to the Garden from the run of the mill. Here the means of production, the quality of the food, its authenticity and provenance count

for everything and there is a genuine curiosity and delight in sourcing new producers. They stock their own Astley Estate organic meat and game, Mrs. Temple's cheese, Cley Smokehouse fish and when available organic vegetables from the Camphill Community at Thornage, only a couple miles away. For more than six months of the year, their organic sheep and cattle roam on the meadows of the River Stiffkey, which is also home to deer, game, rare wildlife and flora.

"We are proud to cook so much of our delicatessen food in our kitchens and not to have to buy in our ready meals, but make them on site from our organic meat and vegetables," says head chef, Brian Brooks. The café food can be enjoyed under the ceiling of massive eighteenth-century oak, or if it's warm, amongst the flowers in the garden. Haddock chowder, rack of lamb, braised pork belly, puy lentil dhal, carrot cake and lightly spiced poached fruit crumble are a few of the delicious dishes you might find. They run two menus side-by-side, one full of all-year-round dishes, and the other a constantly changing and seasonally focused celebration of the best of the week or even day!

Back to the Garden

Back to the Garden
SUMMER CHICKEN SALAD

In this recipe we use organic chicken breast from Astley Farm, we also use fresh produce from the vegetable counter in our shop which is always varied and exciting.

Preparation time: 15 minutes | Cooking time: 40 minutes | Serves 4

Ingredients

4 organic free-range chicken breasts, skin on

650g new potatoes

500g tenderstem broccoli

1 bunch of Norfolk asparagus

Salt and pepper

1 fresh red chilli, diced

1 red onion, diced

For the rub:

½ tsp fennel seeds

½ tsp cumin seeds

½ tsp ground black pepper

½ tsp coriander seeds

½ tsp garlic powder

20g paprika

½ tsp cayenne pepper

50g soft dark brown sugar

25g granulated sugar

½ tsp rosemary, diced

50g malted salt

For the dressing:

1 tbsp Dijon mustard

1 tbsp Norfolk honey

1 tbsp cider vinegar

6-8 tbsp vegetable oil

Salt and pepper to taste

Method

Preheat the oven to 180°c.

Put all the rub ingredients into a food processor or bar blender and blitz into a fine powder.

Take the chicken breasts and coat in olive oil before covering completely with the rub.

In a hot pan, colour both sides of the chicken until golden brown, then place them in the oven for 14-16 minutes.

Place the potatoes in a pan cover with salted water and bring to the boil until soft.

In a separate saucepan bring some salted water to the boil. Meanwhile, trim the base off the asparagus and tenderstem broccoli.

Add these to the water for around 2-3 minutes, leaving the vegetables hard in the centre.

Place them in a bowl with a drizzle of olive oil and season, put in a hot dry pan to colour - this will only take a couple of seconds.

Slice the new potatoes and using the same pan, sauté until coloured. Add these to the other vegetables along with the chilli and red onion.

Make the dressing by adding the mustard, honey and cider vinegar into a bowl. Slowly add the oil whilst whisking the mixture together, season to taste.

To serve

Add the dressing to the vegetables and potato mix, lightly toss and place at the bottom of the serving dish.

Remove the chicken from the oven and rest on the side for 2 minutes. Slice and serve on top of the salad, spooning some of the juices from the tray over for added flavour.

Back to the Garden
TRIO OF SCOTCH EGGS

Our pork comes from a small farm down the road and is prepared by our butcher Paul who makes Cumberland style sausage meat. For something a bit different, here are two additional types of Scotch eggs to try out. The eggs are free-range with bright and shiny yolks!

Preparation time: 20 minutes | Cooking time: 10 minutes | Serves 9

Ingredients

9 large eggs

For the traditional Scotch eggs:

1kg Back To The Garden Cumberland sausage meat

For the veggie Scotch eggs:

2 peppers, diced

1 red onion, diced

8 chestnut mushrooms, diced

5 medium carrots, grated

300g breadcrumbs

3 large eggs

100g pumpkin seeds

100g pine nuts

70g walnuts

Handful of chopped parsley

For the mackerel Scotch eggs:

12 fillets of smoked mackerel

1 tbsp horseradish

1 large egg

1 egg yolk

Pinch of dill

Salt and pepper to taste

For the breadcrumbs:

400g flour

5 large eggs, beaten

500g breadcrumbs

Method

Start by putting nine eggs in a pan of boiling water for no more than 6½ minutes, then plunge them straight into ice cold water.

Once cold, peel the eggs carefully to not break them.

Mix all the ingredients together for your chosen Scotch egg mixture, weigh out 115g of it and mould into a disc.

Coat an egg in plain flour and wrap in the mixture making sure it's well covered.

Coat it in flour once again then dip it in the egg before rolling in breadcrumbs.

Repeat the whole process for all 9 eggs, and then refrigerate them for 15-20 minutes.

Preheat the oven to 180°c and heat a deep fryer to 190°c

Place into the fryer for 5 minutes then into the oven for 4 minutes. Rest for 2 minutes before serving.

Showcasing NORFOLK

Since it opened in 2015, Benedicts has been taking the incredible produce of the county and giving it a unique platform to shine in stunning seasonal cooking.

When Benedicts first opened its doors in the centre of Norwich, it encapsulated everything that chef owner Richard Bainbridge and his wife Katja loved in a restaurant. Having gained national recognition at Morston Hall and from his appearance on BBC's Great British Menu, there was much speculation and excitement surrounding Richard's first solo venture.

The idea behind Benedicts, which is based on arty St Benedicts Street, was simple: "We wanted to create a restaurant that we wished existed – it was going to be a place that we loved," Richard explains.

The inspiration comes from the county he calls home and he simply cannot shout loud enough about all the amazing small producers in Norfolk. Everything Richard serves in Benedicts is locally sourced, and he likes to use his dishes to showcase the incredible array of produce, giving it the culinary platform it deserves.

When people come here, Richard hopes to give them a sense of what Norfolk is about. Diners should be able to locate themselves in a time and place from the plate of food in front of them – for example, one mouthful can tell a diner that this is Norfolk in the spring.

However, Richard and Katja agree there is so much more to hospitality than excellent food. The plate may tell the diner that they are well and truly in Norfolk, but so should the genuine friendliness and warmth when they enter the restaurant. It's about the whole experience. Their honest approach has helped them to become so successful, and they have been welcomed by the people of Norwich as well as diners who have travelled to the city to sample the food.

From two employees when they opened to a total of 18 staff today, it has been quite a whirlwind experience! Richard has been supported in the kitchen by sous chef Ashley Williamson from day one, and Ashley has been hugely important throughout the journey so far. They have also welcomed general manager Adam Vass on board, who has been a key player in the team, helping to drive the business forward on a daily basis.

"Every member of the team shares the values that we have had from the start," says Richard, "great food, great wine, great atmosphere."

Benedicts
BETTY IN THE HEN HOUSE

Show-stopping dish created for the BBC's Great British Menu 2015. The barley needs to be soaked overnight before cooking. Ask your butcher to prepare the quails for you.

Preparation time: 45 minutes, plus overnight soaking | Cooking time: 1 hour 30 | Serves 4

Ingredients

For the stuffing:

1kg sausage meat

150g diced back fat

75g chicken liver, trimmed, cleaned and diced

1 small shallot, chopped

1 clove of garlic, sweated down

1 jar of chutney of your choice

1 tsp French mustard

Salt and pepper

25g each of chervil, parsley and tarragon, finely chopped

For the quails:

4 quails, deboned from the bottom up and trimmed of any excess fat

For the chicken jus:

500g chicken bones

2 shallots, 1 carrot and 1½ sticks celery, chopped

500ml white wine, plus a splash for finishing

1 litre each veal and chicken stock

1½ garlic cloves

1 sprig of thyme

1 bay leaf

Small knob of butter

5g each flat leaf parsley, chervil and chives, chopped

For the pearl barley:

125g salted butter

½ leek, thinly sliced

100g pearl barley, soaked overnight in water

125ml white wine

1 litre chicken stock, boiling

30g Parmesan cheese, grated

¼ bunch flat leaf parsley, finely chopped

½ bunch chervil, finely chopped

Method

For the stuffing

Preheat the oven to 180°c. Place all the stuffing ingredients into a large bowl and mix well. Fry off a small piece to check for seasoning. Place the quail onto the surface with the front of the bird looking at you. Place a small amount of the stuffing into the legs and a small sausage in the middle of the bird, using a trussing needle sew the bird back up. Using more string tie the bird back up so it looks like an oven-ready bird.

Place a pan onto a high heat, season the bird with salt and seal all over until golden. Place in the preheated oven for 10-12 minutes. Remove from oven and let rest for 20-30 minutes. Remove the string before serving.

For the chicken jus

Place a medium pot on a high heat, add the chicken bones and fry off until golden brown. Remove from the pot and repeat with the chopped vegetables. Place the roasted chicken bones back in the pot with the vegetables and add the white wine. Bring to the boil and reduce by three-quarters. Add the two different stocks, garlic, thyme and bay leaf. Bring to the boil, then turn down to a simmer and skim. Cook the sauce out for about 45 minutes. Pass through muslin into a clean pot, return to a high heat and reduce to the consistency you want. To finish the sauce add a splash of white wine, a small knob of butter and the chopped parsley, chervil and chives.

For the pearl barley

Place a large pot onto a medium heat, add 25g of the butter and the leek and slowly start to sweat off. Once fully cooked add the pearl barley and white wine. Let the white wine reduce by three-quarters. Add enough chicken stock to cover and stir well. Let the barley cook a little like risotto; after 5 minutes add more stock and continue in this way until the barley is soft and tender. To finish, add the rest of the butter and the Parmesan, and stir well. At the last moment add the herbs. Check the seasoning.

To serve

Arrange the pearl barley on the plate and top with the quail, your choice of vegetables and the chicken jus.

We dont sell bicycles,
SORRY

From the first breakfast to the last cocktail, The Bicycle Shop is here for you.

The Bicycle Shop began in 2009, sitting on St Benedicts Street in the heart of the Norwich Lanes. The name references the history of the building as a bicycle sale and repair shop for 82 years providing the people of Norwich with a means of stable and clean transportation. Now? It provides the people of Norwich with a means of stable and clean lubrication - a place for eating, drinking, music and merriment.

Tyres, chains and bells have been replaced by cake, organic beer and freshly brewed coffee. However, in memory of the old bicycle shop, vintage cycling posters, bike-wheel lampshades and an old bicycle outside decorates the warm and cosy setting. There's a number of reasons why The Bicycle Shop is so inviting, they shop locally, organically and fair-trade, they try to minimise their impact on the environment and they only pick suppliers that they know and trust including Howard & Son fishmongers and Swannington Farm to Fork who pride themselves on livestock that are happy, healthy and drug-free.

Open from morning until late at night, they operate on three floors. The basement used for drinking, live music, poetry, film screenings and DJ nights.

Dark and tempting, The Handle Bar has absinthe fountains on the bar, draught beers and excellent spirits. The other two floors have evolved into comfortable places for brunch, lunch, afternoon tea, big suppers and late night tapas.

From dippy eggs & soldiers, shakshuka and Greek salads to quesadillas, lamb burgers and tagines, you can be sure to find something on their chalkboards each day that will excite the taste buds and satisfy your stomach. For those with a sweet tooth, choose from a selection of scrumptious cakes, puddings and ice creams. Amy, their cake maker, has been producing a wonderful array of baked goods for the last 5 years. Her gluten-free chocolate brownies are so good they have become a permanent fixture.

Filled with local artwork, leafy plants and mismatched furniture, The Bicycle Shop has created an environment to linger in for longer than intended. It's a place to hide. To celebrate. A shared community.

Bicycle Shop

BLACK PUDDING, BACON AND POTATO HASH WITH SPINACH AND POACHED EGGS

This is a firm favourite here; it's been a staple on the menu for years and is as popular as ever. Hearty and restorative, it's a real cure-all. The key is proper coarse black pudding from the butchers and runny yolks - and a Bloody Mary on the side, obviously.

Preparation time: 10 minutes | Cooking time: 20 minutes | Serves 4

Ingredients

Splash of white wine vinegar

1 tbsp butter

½ red onion, thinly sliced

500g new potatoes, halved and parboiled

8 rashers of bacon, thinly sliced

400g black pudding

200g fresh spinach

8 fresh eggs

Salt and pepper

4 slices of sourdough

Method

Dash some white wine vinegar into a pan of water and slowly bring to the boil.

In wide heavy-bottomed pan, melt the butter before adding in the onion and potatoes - cook until the onion is crisp.

Add the bacon and cook until golden. Then crumble in the black pudding, moving regularly until it darkens.

Crack the eggs into the water pan on a steady low rolling boil. Poach for 3 minutes. Meanwhile, toast and butter the slices of sourdough.

Stir the fresh spinach into the hash and season to taste.

Divide the mixture between four bowls and top with two eggs each.

Serve with the toasted sourdough and some organic brown sauce.

A spot of TEA

Biddy's was opened in 2011 by Charlie Buchan who was inspired by the independent business scene down the Norwich Lanes and all of the amazing coffee shops Norwich has to offer.

Charlie wanted to provide an alternative to coffee but still create a homely and fun setting with Victorian-style charm. "It's inspired by my nan and her amazing ability to bring out large portions of afternoon tea for any of my relations when they visited. I thought that I should keep it a bit tongue-in-cheek and full of fun like my nan and it's named after my scruffy dog Biddy to play up to the ironic vintage vibe I wanted to create," says Charlie.

The two venues in Norwich and Aylsham specialise in loose-leaf tea, serving over 60 different variations although there are even more possibilities as customers are encouraged to create their own blend by mixing bases and flavours together. All of their scrumptious cakes are baked in-house by their talented team in the Aylsham kitchen; they also make their own scones, soups, Scotch eggs, sausage rolls, chutneys and jams! Anything they are unable to make themselves they source from local suppliers including vegan cakes from Deerly Beloved, pork pies from Bray's, meat from Pickerings & Coxfords and veg from S&M Brett.

The infamous Biddy's afternoon tea is created by the customer - you choose the sandwiches, the scone, the cake and the tea, and the friendly staff will plate and tier it up for you. All sandwiches are made to order and there are plenty of vegan and gluten-free options too. Their cakes tend to sell out daily with favourites such as banoffee millionaires shortbread, pistachio, geranium & raspberry bakewell and spiced apple crumble cake - the bakers like to get creative and take risks so there's always something new at Biddy's.

For a Mad Hatters tea party like no other, you can have the entire shop to yourselves in the after-hours with your own hostess, vintage parlour games and afternoon tea buffet! Tuesdays is their event day starting with Sugar Tits in the morning which is exclusively for mums and young babies, followed by either a Stitch & Bitch night for any craft and knitting enthusiasts, a Swishing event where people can swap unwanted clothes or the Great Biddy's Bake Off where they welcome aspiring bakers to bring in their masterpieces.

Biddy's seem to have it all covered but if even that's not enough, their sister company Ophelia Weddings design and make bespoke cakes for special occasions.

Biddy's Tearoom
LEMON, TEA AND BISCUIT CHEESECAKE

This recipe incorporates some of our favourite Biddy's dishes. The base is from our millionaire's shortbread, the lemon layer from our squidgy lemon bars and a cold set cheesecake and shortbread to set it off, we prepare everything except the shortbread the day before. We have added our Biddy's Blend loose leaf tea, it is a black Earl Grey base made with half Assam and half Ceylon. This tea is in each layer of the slice giving this lemon square a decidedly Biddy's twist!

Preparation time: 30 minutes and chill overnight | Cooking time: 2 hours | Serves 4

Ingredients

For the biscuit base:

200g plain flour

90g soft brown sugar, light

70g desiccated coconut

Handful of Biddy's Blend tea

190g unsalted butter

For the lemon layer:

6 eggs

550g caster sugar

Zest of 2 lemons, unwaxed

6 lemons, juiced

1 tsp vanilla extract

1 tsp Bergamot essence

100g plain flour, sifted

For the Biddy's blend cheesecake:

1 sheet gelatine

200ml double cream

500g full fat cream cheese

100g icing sugar, sifted

1 vanilla pod or 1 tsp vanilla extract

1 tsp rose essence

1 tsp bergamot essence

Zest of 1 lemon

For the shortbread:

100g butter

50g caster sugar

150g plain flour

1 tsp Bergamot essence

1 tbsp Biddy's Blend tea

To decorate:

Dried edible flowers

Whipping cream

Method

Start by preheating the oven to 160˚c. Then grease and line an 18cm square tin, a loose-based one will make removal easier.

For the biscuit base

Mix all the dry ingredients together in a bowl. Then melt the butter and add it to the dry ingredients to combine. Press the mixture into the bottom of the tin and bake until golden brown, this should take around 10 minutes.

For the lemon layer

In a large bowl mix together the eggs, sugar and lemon zest on high speed, slowly add the lemon juice and essences before turning the speed down and mixing in the flour.

Pour the mixture onto your biscuit base cook for 1-1½ hours. The lemon layer will be set on the top and have a chewy crust. When you shake it there should be a wobble, but it shouldn't be too wet.

For the Biddy's Blend cheesecake

Melt the gelatine in 2 tablespoons of water, meanwhile lightly whip the double cream in a bowl.

In a separate bowl, beat together the cream cheese, icing sugar and vanilla pod seeds or vanilla extract, then fold in the whipped cream along with essences, bloomed gelatine and lemon zest. Spoon the cheesecake mixture over the lemon layer and leave in a fridge overnight.

For the shortbread

Mix all the ingredients together in a bowl before rolling out onto a work surface until it is 1cm in thickness.

Cut out small circular cookie disks and place on a lined baking tray, cool these in a fridge for an hour and then blind bake in the oven until golden brown. Depending on your oven it should take 10-20 minutes.

To serve

Remove the cheesecake from the fridge and use a hot knife to loosen the sides before removing the tin. If using a loose-based tin, rest on an upturned bowl and slide edges down. Cut into neat rectangular slices using a hot knife and decorate with a piped Chantilly cream swirl. Place a shortbread biscuit on top and sprinkle over some dried edible flowers and loose leaf Biddy's Blend tea.

The heart of
THE VILLAGE

When Russell and Clare Evans bought their local pub, The Boars, Spooner Row, their aim was to create an inviting space for the whole community to come together – good beers, great food and a warm welcome.

Russell and Clare had been living near The Boars, Spooner Row for 20 years when they decided to buy it, so they had all the knowledge at their fingertips to really make it into a place that the whole community would cherish.

One thing they appreciated from the start was just how vital the people of Spooner Row and the surrounding villages would be to their business. The pub is an essential place for villagers to get together so this has always been at the forefront of their plans. With this in mind, they kept The Snug 'dog-friendly', as well as the garden of course, and have developed a great 'little piglets' menu for children, so families can bring the little ones along, too.

However, they also wanted to make The Boars, Spooner Row into a dining destination, and key to this was bringing the two Marks into the team.

Mark Bryant joined as Operations Director, with an eye for detail acquired through a career that took him all over the country before returning to his home county. With experience at the Pheasant Hotel in Kelling and The Globe Inn in Wells-next-the-Sea under his belt, he set about making it into the choice destination for people to visit in Norfolk.

Head chef Mark Elvin had also worked all over the country, and he was drawn back to Norfolk thanks to its incredible natural larder. Having worked at The Wildebeest, he had plenty of experience of creating menus based on Norfolk's rich bounty.

"I think we have some of the best ingredients in the country right here on our doorstep," says Mark, "I love Cromer crab, asparagus when it is in season and all our local game. Here at The Boars we use many local suppliers such as The Paddocks in Bunwell for our meat, and eggs from Cavick Farm at Wymondham. I'm always keen to hear from possible producers, as we like to support them and they offer us something a little different."

From pub classics such as The Boars beef burger, Bunwell bangers and mash or Bullards beer-battered catch of the day to creatively inspired dishes like oven-roasted black bream fillet or slow-cooked rosemary sea salted duck leg, the commitment to quality runs through every single dish.

The Boars

CURRIED MONKFISH TAIL, CAULIFLOWER COUSCOUS, CHARRED LITTLE GEM AND APRICOT PURÉE

Once described as a poor man's lobster, monkfish now features on many a fine dining restaurant menu. I love monkfish because of its meaty firm flesh, versatility and how its robustness works with rich flavours. Paired with curry and sweet apricots, nutty cauliflower, smoky charred lettuce and crisp pomegranate it creates a balanced dish packing a punch.

Preparation time: 30 minutes | Cooking time: 30 minutes | Serves 4

Ingredients

For the monkfish tail:

1kg monkfish tail

4 tbsp Madras curry powder

20g salted butter

1 bunch fresh coriander, finely chopped

1 bunch fresh parsley, finely chopped

Salt and pepper

For the apricot purée:

250g dried apricots

250ml cold water

For the cauliflower couscous:

1 medium-sized cauliflower

2 banana shallots, finely diced

To serve:

1 pomegranate

2 little gem lettuce

28 blanched whole almonds

Method

For the monkfish tail

Prepare the monkfish tail by removing it from the bone and trimming any dark skin, revealing a pink membrane that also needs to be pulled away. Roll out some cling film and sprinkle the Madras curry powder equally on it. Coat the monkfish in the curry powder and roll in the cling film tightly to form a cylinder shape. Set aside for later.

For the apricot purée

Place the apricots and the water in a saucepan and bring to the boil. Simmer for 12 minutes. The apricots will puff up and take on the water. Blitz in a food processor until silky smooth and season to taste.

For the cauliflower couscous

Take the outer leaves from the cauliflower and remove the florets from the stalk. Place the florets in a food processor and pulse until the size and consistency of couscous. Mix the cauliflower with the shallots and sauté for 4-5 minutes, until translucent but not coloured. Season and set aside.

To finish and serve

Cut the pomegranate in half and with a spoon tap the outer skin to remove the pods/seeds. Quarter the little gem lettuce and fry in a hot pan until slightly charred. Add the almonds and fry until golden. Season the almonds with salt.

Bring a pan of water to the boil, add the rolled monkfish (in the cling film) and gently poach for 5 minutes. Then remove from the water and remove the cling film. Sauté the seasoned monkfish in a hot frying pan with the butter for around 1 minute, coating with the foaming butter while browning.

Once the monkfish is cooked, roll it in the chopped coriander and parsley to coat evenly. Slice the monkfish and serve with the cauliflower couscous, apricot purée, pomegranate, salted almonds and little gem lettuce.

Flawless dining EXPERIENCE

Brasted's is a multi award-winning restaurant, catering and events company, with over 30 years' experience serving royalty, dignitaries, celebrities and guests from all over the world.

The name Brasted's is synonymous with fine dining in Norfolk. Located in the picturesque privately owned village of Framingham Pigot, Brasted's enjoys a superb setting in the heart of the Norfolk countryside, but just 4 miles from Norwich city centre.

Brasted's boasts a 2 AA rosette restaurant, which has recently undergone an extensive refurbishment, a 5 AA star boutique B & B and their own wedding and event suite. For a breathtaking alternative venue in Norfolk, Brasted's also offers exclusive hire of the magnificent and historic Langley Abbey.

Brasted's award-winning restaurant has recently undergone a dramatic refurbishment, so the lavish surroundings now reflect the sublime dishes and renowned service for which they are so well known.

From the Louis Vuitton and Villeroy & Boch furnishings to the sparkling glassware and opulent china, every aspect of the surroundings has been meticulously considered to create a dining experience like no other in Norfolk.

Executive chef and director Chris 'Buzz' Busby works his magic in the kitchen, creating seasonally inspired and locally sourced Norfolk menus. He features traditional British dishes with a modern European twist, such as hand dived king scallops, crisp artichoke, cauliflower snow, avocado and sicilian lemon emulsion for starters or Swannington's beef fillet, bone marrow and shallot crust, cauliflower gratin, straw potato rosti and chorizo goulash for the main course. He also particularly enjoys using Norfolk game during the shooting season, such as grouse, mallard and partridge.

However, it isn't just the food that has been racking up the accolades over the years. The multi award-winning front of house team are on-hand to ensure that every aspect of your dining experience is flawless.

The philosophy at Brasted's is 'great company, fabulous food and wonderful wines, as often as possible', which embodies everything they continue to strive for. With this in mind, whatever the occasion, you are guaranteed a memorable experience at Brasted's restaurant.

Brasted's
RILLETTES OF CROMER CRAB

You will need to prepare the pickled vegetables 24 hours in advance, as well as preparing the avocado sorbet in time to allow it to freeze.

Preparation time: 1 hour, plus chilling, freezing and pickling | Cooking time: 20 minutes | Serves 4

Ingredients

For the pickled vegetables:

100ml white wine vinegar

100g sugar

1 carrot

1 parsnip

1 red pepper

1 yellow pepper

For the rillettes:

2 freshly dressed Cromer crab

Pinch of paprika

1 tsp lemon juice

Salt and pepper

50g salted butter

For the sweetcorn panna cotta:

250ml double cream

200g tinned sweetcorn

Salt

1 leaf of gelatine, soaked in cold water

For the avocado sorbet:

1 vanilla pod, halved

½ lemon, zest and juice

½ lime, zest and juice

100g caster sugar

4 ripe avocados

500ml whole milk

For the samphire tempura:

100g trimmed samphire

85g plain flour

½ tsp salt

½ tsp sugar

200ml sparkling water

Oil, for deep-frying

Method

For the pickled vegetables

Put the white wine vinegar and sugar into heavy-bottomed pan, bring to the boil and simmer for 5 minutes. Remove from the heat and leave to cool until cold. Cut the vegetables into your desired shapes (strips, ribbons, balls, etc), place them into the cooled pickling liquid and leave for 24 hours.

For the rillettes

Scrape the dressed crabs from their shells into a bowl, making sure you do not have any pieces of shell in the meat. Dust with the paprika, add the lemon juice and salt and pepper. Melt the butter and drizzle over the crab. Use a fork to gently mix into a rough paste. Place in an airtight container and chill.

For the sweetcorn panna cotta

Place the double cream in a heavy-bottomed pan, add the sweetcorn and place on a low heat for 10 minutes. Season to taste, then blitz in a liquidizer for 1 minute until smooth, strain, add the gelatine and pour into moulds. Chill for 2 hours.

For the avocado sorbet

Scrape the seeds from the vanilla pod into a small saucepan and place the scraped pod in as well. Add the lemon, lime and sugar, and place on a low heat to dissolve the sugar and create a syrup. Leave to cool. Put the avocado flesh into a liquidizer with the milk and syrup, discarding the vanilla pod, and liquidise until smooth. Churn in an ice cream machine then freeze.

For the samphire tempura

Heat the oil for deep-frying. Thoroughly wash the samphire and dry with a cloth. Place the flour, salt and pepper into a bowl, pour over the sparkling water and mix into a batter. Dip the samphire into the batter and deep-fry until crisp.

To serve

Remove the rillettes and panna cotta from the fridge and remove the sorbet from the freezer. Serve with the pickled vegetables and samphire tempura.

Brasted's
ROASTED LOIN
OF HOLKHAM VENISON

The venison needs to be marinated for 24 hours for the best flavour, and the pickled celeriac will also need 24 hours of pickling, so this recipe needs to be started a day in advance.

Preparation time: 30 minutes, plus pickling and marinating | Cooking time: 40 minutes | Serves 4

Ingredients

For the venison:

1kg venison loin

200ml rapeseed oil

2 garlic cloves

2 sprigs thyme

For the pickled celeriac:

100ml white wine vinegar

100g sugar

3 star anise

1 whole celeriac

For the potato cylinders:

2 good-sized jacket potatoes

Butter, for cooking

Salt and pepper

For the foraged woodshrooms:

100g wild mushrooms

50g butter

Salt and pepper

Dash of sherry

To serve:

Roasted carrots and buttered kale

Method

For the venison

Place the venison on a chopping board and remove any sinew and fat. Put the rapeseed oil in a liquidizer with the garlic and thyme, and liquidise for 1 minute until all the contents are smooth. Now you have your marinade. Cover the venison in the marinade and leave for 24 hours or as long as possible.

For the pickled celeriac

Place the white wine vinegar, sugar and star anise into heavy-bottomed pan, bring to the boil and simmer for 5 minutes. Remove from the heat and leave to cool. Cut the celeriac into your desired shapes (strips, ribbons, balls, etc), then place them into the cooled pickling liquid. Leave for 24 hours.

For the potato cylinders

Peel the potatoes and cut the top and bottom off. Using an apple corer, cut cylinders all the way through, just like you would with an apple. Once you have your cylinders, you need to cook them until soft, then put in a frying pan over medium heat and baste with butter until coloured. Season and set aside.

For the foraged woodshrooms

Heat a frying pan, toss in the butter and mushrooms and sauté for 30 seconds. Splash in the sherry, season and serve straight away.

To serve

Roast the venison until cooked to your liking and serve with the pickled celeriac, potato cylinders, foraged woodshrooms and some roasted carrots and buttered kale.

True TRANQUILITY

With its beautiful coastal location and comfortable rooms, Briarfields is a hidden gem on the coast – the perfect place to enjoy a short break or a taste of Norfolk life.

Briarfields enjoys a spectacular setting on the north-west Norfolk coast, tucked away from the hustle and bustle in a tranquil spot overlooking the sea and salt marshes. The Norfolk chalk building is surrounded by wide open spaces with uninterrupted views of the countryside around.

Step inside and this family-owned hotel oozes character and charm thanks to the attention to detail that has gone into the contemporary styling. A roaring fire and log burners provide warmth during winter and there are numerous cosy spots for guests to curl up with a newspaper or a book after a day exploring the Norfolk coast. During the summer, stylish decking looks out to the sea and salt marshes, making it an ideal spot for a glass of Pimm's in the afternoon.

With such a remarkable landscape on their doorstep, the team at Briarfields is constantly inspired by the natural larder of the county around them. This can be seen in their seasonal approach to food, as well as their passion for local produce. Freshly caught fish and locally sourced meat take centre stage, with vegetarian options and freshly prepared children's dishes alongside. The creative menu is beautifully prepared and presented, and they are well-known for their selection of homemade desserts.

The afternoon at Briarfields is perhaps the favourite part of the day for many guests, thanks to the beautifully presented delectable afternoon tea. The hotel's staff aim to make this traditional British affair a little bit of luxury for diners, complete with classic sandwiches, scones with jam and cream, and mouthwatering mini desserts.

The award-winning hotel is listed in The Good Hotel Guide 2017 thanks to its winning combination of relaxed ambience and top-quality service. The mix of areas caters for all occasions – a homely snug with a roaring fire to enjoy the tranquility away from it all, a TV lounge with Sky and plenty of games for families to enjoy, and an outside play area too. In keeping with Norfolk's love of man's best friend, dogs are welcome in the hotel and in a number of its bedrooms.

Whether it's a romantic break, spending time with family, escaping for a rural retreat, tucking into seasonal Norfolk cuisine or visiting for a sumptuous afternoon tea, Briarfields aims to provide the perfect atmosphere to eat, drink, relax and get away from it all.

briarfields HOTEL

eat

Briarfields
PAN-FRIED CURRIED LOCH DUARTE SUPREME OF SALMON, BUTTERED LEEKS AND SAFFRON POTATOES

Salmon is a favourite fish for many, but by adding new flavours with spice, this dish elevates the everyday into something extraordinary. By using a mild Madras curry powder on the skin of the salmon, along with accent flavours such as saffron, yoghurt and coriander, it takes the salmon in a new direction, enhancing its overall flavour without destroying the underlying texture and taste of the fish.

Preparation time: 20 minutes | Cooking time: 20 minutes | Serves 2

Ingredients

200g natural yoghurt

½ bunch fresh coriander, roughly chopped

Mild curry powder, to coat

2 x 170g (6 oz.) pieces of Loch Duarte salmon

12 new potatoes, cooked and cut in half

50g butter

1 small packet of saffron

1 small leek, cut in half lengthways and diced

Salt and pepper

Vegetable oil, for cooking

Method

Preheat the oven to 180°c. Put the natural yoghurt into a small bowl, then mix in the chopped coriander. Place in the fridge.

Fill a large saucepan two-thirds full of water and place on a high heat. Put a medium-sized frying pan on a medium heat with a little oil, enough to cover the bottom of the pan.

Place a little of the curry powder into a small bowl, coat the salmon on the skin side and shake off any excess. Place the salmon carefully into the frying pan skin-side down and leave for 2-3 minutes until golden brown. Carefully turn the salmon over and cook for 1 minute until sealed. Take the salmon out of the pan and place on a tray skin-side up. Place in the oven for 8-10 minutes.

While the salmon is cooking place the cooked halved potatoes in the boiling water for 3-5 minutes or until hot. In a separate small saucepan melt half of the butter and put a generous pinch of saffron into the butter until the saffron infuses with the butter and changes colour. Add the potatoes to the pan until they take on the colour of the saffron. Add a pinch of salt and pepper and keep warm.

Take the salmon out of the oven and keep warm. Place the leeks into the pan of boiling water for 2 minutes, or until just cooked. Drain the leeks, add the rest of the butter, season with salt and pepper and keep warm.

Divide the saffron potatoes between two plates, placing them just off centre. Place the leeks at the side of the potatoes. Place the salmon on top, put a spoonful of the coriander yoghurt on the salmon and serve.

Beautifully QUIRKY

A well-known fixture of Holt's picturesque town centre is the handsome 19th-century brick and flint building that is home to Byfords posh B&B, café and store.

Just off the High Street, the eye-catching Byfords building is beloved in Holt. Thought to be one of the oldest buildings in the town, its handsome exterior gives way to a quirky warren of nooks and crannies inside. It creates an intriguing space that the owners describe as "a higgledy piggledy world of pleasure", containing a takeaway store, 120-seat café and posh B&B.

The building itself began life as a family hardware business run by Henry Byford. Although the hardware store is no more, the Byford name lives on in the current Byfords business. Byfords as we now know it opened in 2000 when Iain and Clair Wilson, a pair of local entrepreneurs, opened the café, store and B&B. They both had backgrounds in hospitality, but they admit that they had no idea just how successful the business would become.

They put Norfolk at the heart of Byfords, which can be seen in the type of food on offer. Local suppliers dominate both the shelves of the store and the dishes served in the café, with fruit, vegetables, eggs and cheeses coming from nearby whenever possible. All the beef and lamb comes from Duncan Jeary, whose animals are reared less than 5 miles away from Byfords. Pork and sausages are sourced from Perfick Pork at Gt Ryburgh, and they get their fresh blood black pudding from Matt and Grant at the award-winning Fruit Pig Company. The Norfolk coastline allows them to use local fisherman for crabs in summer and they adore the smoked haddock and kippers they buy from Cley Smokehouse.

Relying on local produce has a huge impact on the menu, which makes the most of the best produce each season offers. As well as being inspired by the seasons, the dishes are also created to reflect what people like to eat – simple, unfussy and hearty food!

Being a relaxed and family-friendly place has made Byfords a popular spot for people of all ages and at all times of day – including the Duchess of Cambridge who is occasionally seen popping in for a prawn sandwich and slice of Victoria sponge!

Byfords

Byfords
SEAFOOD BOARD

This board contains hot and crispy calamari, smoked mackerel paté, focaccia bread and tartare sauce. The calamari needs to be served immediately.

Preparation time: 1 hour, plus 2 hours proving | Cooking time: 50 minutes | Serves 6

Ingredients

50g Smoked Salmon

For the focaccia:

750g bread flour

15g salt

37g fresh yeast

540ml cold water

210ml olive oil, plus extra for drizzling

Semolina, for sprinkling

Rock salt, for sprinkling

For the smoked mackerel paté:

400g smoked mackerel, skinned and deboned

300g low-fat cream cheese

2 lemons, zest and juice

½ bunch fresh flat-leaf parsley, washed, leaves picked and chopped

3 tsp capers, chopped

For the tartare sauce:

500g mayonnaise

40g capers

1 lemon, zest and juice

50g baby cornichons, chopped

15 fresh parsley, chopped

For the calamari:

90g self-raising flour

8g Cajun seasoning

8g hot chilli powder

5g salt

5g cracked black pepper

3 fresh squid (cartilage removed from the centre, then sliced into rings)

Oil, for deep-frying

Method

For the focaccia

Tip the flour into a large mixing bowl with the salt and mix for 1 minute. Dissolve the yeast into three-quarters of the water, then add this to the flour, along with all of the olive oil and turn the mixture around with your fingers. Continue to add water, a little at a time, until you have picked up all the flour from the sides of the bowl. You may not need to add all the water or you may need to add a little extra. You want the dough to be very soft – wetter than a standard bread dough. Use the mixture to clean the inside of the bowl and keep going until a rough dough is formed.

Knead for 8-10 minutes until the dough forms a soft, smooth and elastic mixture (try to avoid adding any extra flour to the mixture). Put the dough into a lightly oiled tub and cover with a tea towel. Leave until doubled in size – this could take up to an hour.

Oil a 2.5cm-deep baking tray. Place the dough onto a surface sprinkled with a little semolina and gently divide the dough into two, trying not to knock any air out of it. Carefully place the dough into the tray, giving enough space for it to double in size. Cover in cling film and allow to double in size again (this could take an hour again).

Preheat the oven to 180°c. Once doubled in size, dip your fingers in oil and prod dimples into the top of the dough, then sprinkle with a little rock salt and drizzle with oil. Bake for 40-50 minutes until golden. The loaf should sound hollow when tapped on the bottom. Turn out on to a wire rack and allow to cool.

For the smoked mackerel paté

Blend the mackerel in a blender until almost smooth. In a separate bowl mix all the other ingredients then mix the mackerel by hand into the cream cheese mixture. Taste and season where necessary. Keep chilled until needed. When serving, place a good spoons worth onto the platter and garnish with cucumber and caper berries.

For the tartare sauce

Place the mayonnaise in a bowl and add the capers, lemon juice, zest and cornichons. Taste and add the parsley, season if required. Keep chilled until needed.

For the calamari

Mix all the dry ingredients together then toss the squid rings through the powder, ensuring they are well coated. Heat the oil for deep-frying to around 170°c. Place the calamari into the fryer and fry for around 2 minutes until crisp and golden. Drain and place onto some paper towels to ensure the calamari does not soak up any oil. Serve immediately.

To Serve

Construct the board combining all the different parts and curl the salmon into a rose to place on top.

Making their
DEBUT

Debut Restaurant is the region's highest rated training facility that allows City College Norwich's hospitality and catering students to experience a real working environment as part of their courses.

Guests at debut can enjoy a unique fine dining experience courtesy of the college's talented student chefs and front of house staff who are following in the footsteps of the likes of Tom Aikens, Richard Bainbridge and Richard Hughes, who all started their careers at the college's Hotel School restaurant.

Debut has built up a loyal following and has a deserved reputation for its warm welcome, excellent cuisine using locally sourced ingredients, and great value for money. It is East Anglia's only training restaurant that holds two Centre of Excellence statuses alongside the top Highly Commended rating from the coveted AA College Rosette Scheme. Their outstanding reputation has seen the team provide catering at a range of high-profile events including The Queen's Diamond Jubilee Garden Party at Sandringham House in 2012.

Over the years, the restaurant has played host to a variety of notable events for a range of local clients and has welcomed some of the biggest names in the hospitality industry including Delia Smith, Ainsley Harriott, Roger Hickman and Albert Roux.

The Hotel School's expert lecturers and exceptional employer links ensure all students are trained to an incredibly high standard which sees many securing employment at some of the industry's most prestigious companies.

Debut Restaurant is based on City College Norwich's Ipswich Road campus and is open for lunch and dinner during term time with regular themed evenings and guest chef events throughout the year.

As well as offering a fine dining experience, the Hotel School also run a range of evening and weekend leisure courses for those who are interested in developing their culinary skills. These range from the Junior Chef Academy, sugar craft, Great British Bake Off, gluten-free masterclass and student cookery on a budget.

City College Norwich is a large, well-established college of further and higher education. In 2016, the college celebrated 125 years of providing its local community and the employers of Norfolk with excellence in vocational education and training, including apprenticeships, as well as academic, higher education and professional courses. Today the college has over 10,000 students and provides excellent preparation for their career development and progression.

Cooking up the
CURRICULUM

Joe Mulhall is the Curriculum Programme Manager of the Hotel School at City College Norwich, where education and cooking go hand in hand.

Joe Mulhall has been the Curriculum Programme Manager in Hotel Hospitality, Catering and Tourism for nine years, but his history with the Hotel School at City College Norwich goes back much further than that, as he actually studied there himself.

He originally applied for the tourism course but was turned down. Luckily, he was interested in cooking too, having come from a family of people who had worked in the food industry. Having seen how the Hotel School helped him develop in both confidence and skills, he knew that he would love to work there one day.

He recalls how studying something that he enjoyed so much transformed him from an average student to becoming Hospitality and Catering Student of the Year within a year. He puts this down not only to the enjoyment he gained from it, but also to the friendships that were forged. As everyone there was interested in food, they would discuss food and drink both in and out of college, and they would enjoy eating out together, too.

After three years of studying his career took him to Germany before coming back to Norfolk to work for Anglia TV, catering for celebrities in the green room, followed by a move to London to work for Channel 4 and Channel 5.

He moved to work for a contract company that revitalised old office, school and college canteens, which eventually led Joe back to City College Norwich. Being back on the college campus was a positive experience for Joe, and when the opportunity arose for a trainer in the Hotel School he couldn't let it pass him by.

Keen to develop within education, he undertook higher levels of learning and teacher training before achieving the role of course leader and eventually stepping up to become Curriculum Programme Manager.

Joe's career development is a shining example of what he thinks the college can help students achieve. No matter what stage chefs or restaurateurs are at in their career, they are continually developing and finding their own style – and this happens from day one at the college.

City College Norwich

MANGO BAVAROIS WITH MANGO SALSA AND COCONUT SORBET

A medley of flavours and textures come together in this exotic dessert.

Preparation time: 1 hour, plus setting, cooling and freezing | Cooking time: 10 minutes | Serves 4-6

Ingredients

For the mango bavarois:

3 egg yolks

105g caster sugar

200ml milk

1 vanilla pod

3½ sheets gelatine, soaked

100g mango purée

150ml double cream

75g egg whites

Pinch of cream of tartar

For the coconut sorbet:

110g caster sugar

400ml can coconut milk

25g desiccated coconut

50ml coconut cream

½ lemon, juice only

1 tbsp coconut liqueur

For the sugared coconut:

1 coconut

100g caster sugar

For the mango and lime salsa:

1 ripe mango

2 limes, zest and juice

8 mint leaves, finely chopped

50g icing sugar

Method

For the mango bavarois

In a heatproof bowl, whisk the egg yolks with 75g of the sugar until pale and creamy. Pour the milk into a saucepan. Cut the vanilla pod lengthwise, scrape the seeds into the milk, and bring to the boil. Pour the boiling milk over the egg yolk mixture, whisking all the time. Place the bowl over a pan of gently simmering water (ensuring that the bottom of the bowl doesn't touch the water) and whisk vigorously for 8-12 minutes, until the mixture thickens and the whisk leaves a trail as it goes through. Remove the bowl from the heat, stir in the soaked gelatine leaves and mango purée, and set over a bowl of ice.

In another bowl, whip the cream with an electric beater until peaks form. In a separate bowl whisk the egg whites, cream of tartar and remaining 30g of sugar to form stiff peaks. When the bavarois is completely cold and firming up, fold the whipped cream and egg whites through until completely incorporated. Place into 4-6 moulds that you can turn out onto a plate when set completely. Place in thr fridge for 2 hours to set.

For the coconut sorbet

Place all the ingredients into a heavy-bottomed pan and heat to a gentle simmer, then remove from the heat and allow to cool for 1 hour at room temperature.

Place the sorbet mixture into a plastic tub and place into the freezer. Mix with a fork every 30 minutes until the mixture starts to thicken and turns a nice white colour, then leave to harden up for an hour. Scoop it out with an ice-cream scoop to serve.

For the sugared coconut

Preheat the oven to 160°c. Crack the coconut shell to reveal the nut inside. Peel the coconut flesh into strips and dust with caster sugar. Place into the oven for 10 minutes or until golden brown. Leave in a cool place until cooled and crispy.

For the mango and lime salsa

Peel the mango and dice into small cubes. Add the lime zest and juice, and finely chopped mint, then fold though the icing sugar. Place into the fridge for 30 minutes to improve the flavour.

City College Norwich

CURRIED SALMON WITH COCONUT LENTIL DHAL, ROAST CAULIFLOWER, SPINACH AND ONION BHAJI CRISPS

Bursting with aromatic spices, this recipe packs a punch when it comes to flavour.

Preparation time: 20 minutes, plus 30 minutes marinating | Cooking time: 1 hour | Serves 4

Ingredients

For the curried salmon:

1 dstspn curry powder

1 dstspn caster sugar

Pinch of salt

4 salmon fillets

1dstspn oil

For the coconut lentil dhal:

2 tbsp olive oil

1 tsp mustard seeds

1 tsp cumin seeds

1 onion, diced

2 garlic cloves, peeled and sliced

½ tsp turmeric

250g red lentils

400g coconut milk

400g chopped tomatoes

1 tbsp chopped coriander

1 tbsp natural yoghurt

For the cauliflower and spinach:

2 bags of spinach

Knob of butter

1 cauliflower

Pinch of salt

Pinch of curry powder

1 dstspn oil

For the onion bhaji crisps:

150g gram flour

1 tsp of each turmeric, paprika, ground coriander, cumin and fennel seeds

1 bunch coriander, chopped

4 red onions, finely sliced

Method

For the curried salmon

Preheat the oven to 180°c. Mix the curry powder, sugar and salt together in a small bowl. Place the fillets of salmon onto a plate then sprinkle the curry powder mix over the salmon and cover in the fridge for 30 minutes. Put the oil in a hot pan and colour the non-skin side of the salmon until it is a nice golden colour, but be careful as if the pan is too hot it will burn the sugar in the curry mix. Once it is coloured, place on a baking tray and cook in the oven for 15 minutes or until it is cooked through.

For the coconut lentil dhal

Heat the oil in a pan and add the mustard seeds and cumin seeds. Cook for 2-3 minutes, until the mustard seeds start to 'pop'. Add the onion and garlic and cook for 3-4 minutes before stirring in the turmeric. Cook for 1 minute.

Pour in the lentils, coconut milk, chopped tomatoes and 100ml water and stir. Season well. Bring to the boil and simmer for 25-30 minutes, stirring occasionally to prevent the lentils from sticking to the bottom of the pan. Just before serving, stir in the coriander and yoghurt.

For the roasted cauliflower and spinach

Preheat the oven to 180°c. Wash the spinach and drain well, then put into a hot pan with a knob of butter. Sauté for 2 minutes and season. Cut the cauliflower into florets, place onto a baking tray, sprinkle with the salt, curry powder and oil, and roast in the preheated oven for 20 minutes until golden brown and crispy.

For the onion bhaji crisps

Half-fill a large pan with vegetable oil and heat to 175°c. In a mixing bowl, stir together the gram flour, all the spices and the chopped coriander. Season to taste. Pour in 150ml cold water, whisking as you go, until you have a thick, gloopy paste. Toss the sliced onions in the batter, and then use tongs to carefully lower small blobs of the onion mixture into the oil. Fry for 3-4 minutes, turning them in the oil every so often, until they are golden and crisp. Remove with a slotted spoon and drain. Drain the bhaji well on kitchen paper.

To serve

Serve the salmon on a bed of dhal, with the cauliflower, spinach and onion bhaji crisps.

Not your run of
THE MILL

True to the name, Cley Windmill is a spectacular windmill, complete with sails. Created in the early 19th century, the unique five-storey venue is a place of true serenity.

Cley Windmill is rich in history; it has seen an abundance of different owners over the years and is now under the watchful eye of Dr Julian Godlee and Carolyn Godlee who have developed it to what it is today. In recent years it has been through an extensive programme of renovation which has paid off as it was listed number one in the 'Four of the Best Places to Stay in Norfolk' article in The Telegraph.

"Every season has something special to offer. In winter, guests really enjoy their bracing muddy walks, comfy squashy sofas in front of the roaring fire, and scrummy plates of food. In summer, they enjoy sipping prosecco in the walled garden, looking out over the reeds to the sea in the distance, and watching the spectacular sunsets. Visitors often say that they feel as though they've escaped and it's lovely to see people unwind and visibly relax," says Carolyn.

Guests can enjoy breathtaking views from the gallery before settling down to dine by candlelight - these are intimate affairs as the venue can seat only 24 in the beamed dining room, although there is the option to have a marquee in the walled garden which can cater for 60 people, perfect for weddings and celebrations!

Their chefs have made quite a name for themselves all over North Norfolk for their cooking which is predominately old-fashioned English country. Each day sees a new set dinner menu which can be tweaked to suit dietary requirements and on Sunday lunchtimes they often serve a traditional roast with your choice of starter and pudding. Chefs Jimmi and Emma work closely together to devise exciting innovative dishes; on one day you could be having Moroccan lamb tagine and the next day you'll be given pan-fried hake with lemon and herb butter sauce!

They pride themselves on providing meals that are fantastic value for money and they are open to non-residents as well. When it comes to food, local produce is imperative, with almost all ingredients locally sourced. Their meat often comes from local Graves butchers, the fish from Weston's fishmongers, and their smoked fish and famous kippers come from the Cley Smokehouse.

The sails, the wind, the views, the reeds, the whole atmosphere and of course the delicious food is the reason why so many people keep coming back to this incredibly special place. Cley Windmill clearly has it all and we're big fans.

Cley Windmill
PAN-FRIED LAMB RUMP

This is not your average pan-fried lamb rump – it's teamed with baby fondant potatoes, spicy butternut squash purée, sprouting broccoli and roasted beetroot. This light lamb dish is perfect for a spring evening's supper. Using the freshest ingredients, it is our pleasure to support the local farmers.

Preparation time: 20 minutes | Marinating time: 6 hours-overnight | Cooking time: 20 minutes | Serves 2

Ingredients

For the lamb:

2 garlic cloves

2 sprigs of sage

2 tbsp olive oil

2 lamb rumps

For the potatoes:

6 small potatoes, peeled

200g butter

2 garlic cloves, peeled and crushed

Salt

2 sprigs of rosemary

2 sprigs of thyme

For the butternut squash purée:

Half a butternut squash

1 red chilli

40g butter

For the roasted beetroot:

2 large beetroots

Sesame/vegetable oil

Salt and pepper

For the sprouting broccoli:

200g sprouting broccoli

20g butter

2 pinches of nutmeg

Salt and pepper

Method

For the marinade

Finely chop the garlic before adding it to a bowl along with the sage and oil. Give it a mix and then use this concoction to cover the lamb, leaving it for up to 6 hours or overnight to marinate.

For the potatoes

Preheat the oven to 190°c.

Slice the butter to cover the base of a pan and add your peeled potatoes. Put the stove on a high heat until the butter begins to bubble over the potatoes.

At this point, add your two garlic cloves along with two pinches of salt, rosemary and thyme. Turn over the potatoes and place the pan into the oven for 20 minutes until golden brown and soft throughout.

For the butternut squash purée

Peel and thinly slice the butternut squash. Boil some water and continue to add this to a pan with the butternut squash, keeping the water at a high heat until the vegetable has softened. Next, blend the squash with the addition of the chilli and butter. To finish, put the purée in a sieve and push it through to eliminate any lumps.

For the lamb

Pan fry the lamb on a high heat until golden all over. Place it in the oven for 10 minutes at 200°c, leaving it to rest for 5 minutes before slicing and serving.

For the roasted beetroot

Boil the beetroots until they are cooked; a fork should go through them with ease. Drain and allow to cool, then peel. Use a melon baller to scoop out five balls, coat with oil and season. Place them on a baking tray and then roast in the oven at 190°c for 10 minutes.

For the sprouting broccoli

Bring a pan of water up to a rolling boil. Chop the ends off the broccoli and slice in half. Once the water is boiling, add the broccoli and cover with a lid. After 2 minutes, strain and put into a hot frying pan with butter, seasoning and nutmeg.

To serve

Plate everything up and garnish the dish with a sprinkling of pomegranate seeds and/or pomegranate flesh.

Tradition with A TWIST

Good old-fashioned service with a smile has been Coxfords Butchers' winning formula for nearly 50 years...

The long-established Coxfords Butchers is run by Johnny and Jason. They are both familiar faces behind the counter, having worked at Coxfords since they left school, so when John Coxford decided to retire after 46 years, Johnny and Jason stepped into his shoes.

The business runs in the blood for both of them: "My grandad was a butcher," says Jason, "and Johnny's dad was actually a butcher at Coxfords too." With a new generation of young butchers leading the business, the people of Aylsham might have wondered if there would be any changes at their favourite local butchers. However Johnny and Jason hold the values of a traditional butchers right at the heart of their business – although they have also provided a few modern twists.

They are both keen cooks and, they happily admit, simply love food. "You need to know how to cook meat to be able to sell it," explains Jason, and there is always a knowledgeable member of the team on-hand to advise customers about how to cook each piece of meat. In a way they see educating people about food as part of their job and for this reason, they place a lot of emphasis on the shop being a friendly, accessible and welcoming place to visit.

They are famous in Aylsham for their stunning window display and the array of locally sourced meats that adorn the counter. They are also particularly known for their award-winning sausages, which claimed a Battle of the Bangers award at the Norfolk Food & Drink Festival in 2016.

Although they love to hand over those prize joints ready for Sunday roasts, they are also aware that lots of people don't have much time in the week to spend hours preparing dinner. For this reason they have increased their product line to include lots of ready-to-cook items, from stir-fry packs to hand-made pizzas, so that customers can enjoy something freshly made when they don't have the time to cook from scratch. There are plenty of allergen-free options too, so do pop in and ask about gluten-free sausages or burgers.

When they are not busy chatting to customers in the shop, the Coxfords team love to put on impressive BBQs or hog roasts for events all over the region. The same top quality of meat and service with a smile is guaranteed!

LAMB SHANKS

THIS WEEK PIGS ARE FROM MR EASEY

BREED:- LARGE WHITES

Battle of the Bangers

This is to certify that

Coxfords Butchers

has been awarded for

WINNER OF THE SPONSORS' CHOICE

in the Battle of the Bangers competition
19 June 2016

norfolkfoodanddrink.com

Norfolk Food & Drink Festival
Battle of the Bangers
The Sponsors Choice
Coxfords Butchers

Coxfords Butchers
QUICK-COOK COTTAGE PIE

This is a simple family meal that makes the most of top-quality local beef mince from Coxfords.

Preparation time: 20 minutes | Cooking time: 30 minutes | Serves 4

Ingredients

4 large potatoes, peeled and chopped into chunks

4 florets of broccoli

4 florets of cauliflower

4 large carrots, peeled and chopped into chunks

1 large onion, chopped

585g good-quality Coxfords beef mince

Dash of Worcestershire sauce

1 tsp horseradish

1 tbsp tomato purée or ketchup

1 tbsp gravy granules, or more if needed

1 tin of peas, drained

Olive oil, for cooking

Butter, for mashing

Method

Put the peeled and chopped potatoes in a pan of boiling water and put the broccoli, cauliflower and carrots in a separate pan of boiling water.

While the vegetables are cooking, fry the onions in a little olive oil until softened. Add the mince and cook to brown. Add the Worcestershire sauce, horseradish and tomato purée or ketchup, then add a cup of water and bring to a simmer. Add the gravy granules to thicken the sauce to your desired consistency.

Check and drain the potatoes, and set aside.

Check and drain the carrots, cauliflower and broccoli and add to the mince, along with the peas.

Mash the potatoes with a little butter and spoon on top of the mince. Put the cottage pie under the grill and cook until browned on top.

Down a winding ROAD

Creake Abbey, known for its atmospheric ruins dating from 1206, lies in a tranquil valley just south of Burnham Market, some ten minutes by car from the north Norfolk coast. This hidden gem is home to a contemporary café and food hall, shops and services located in traditional brick and flint barns, plus an award-winning farmers' market.

A devastating fire occurred at the beginning of the year 1484 followed by plague and pestilence. Today the ancient abbey ruins, steeped in history, are perfect for artists, walkers and those seeking tranquillity. The abbey, once a house of Austin Canons, famous for food provision and care for the local community, is still providing today. Owners Diana and Anthony Scott want to reflect the natural abundance of north Norfolk and bring this to locals and visitors via the farmers' market and through the café and food hall.

Great breakfasts, fine coffee, homemade cakes and scrumptious platters of food are what they are all about and what they hope to tempt visitors with. That and the community of small independent businesses that have been handpicked to create the rural retail destination which has been awarded the Visit England accreditation.

The café strives to use the best local and seasonal ingredients on offer including from Norfolk Saffron and Candi's Chutney to Ethnic Fusion and E H Prior & Son who supply fantastic meat for their crowd-pleasing Sunday roasts and steak nights. Their fishcakes are also a bestseller amongst many other enticing plates which can be enjoyed next to the humongous windows looking out onto the water meadows. It doesn't take long to uncover the fact it's more than just a café.

This picturesque spot is populous with tiny birds, barn owls, geese and other wildlife, perfect for walkers and nature lovers and an ideal site for a rustic wedding venue, art exhibition, gift fairs and their monthly farmers' markets. Over fifty food producers gather each month bringing fresh meat, vegetables, fruits, cheeses, pies, bread, pies and many other goodies – it's the biggest in Norfolk and has won two EDP Norfolk Food & Drink awards for Best Farmers' Market.

Many of these producers supply the food hall where you can find all the bits and bobs you need to cook from scratch or cheat a little on the way! Working with Norfolk cookery writer, Mary Kemp, the food hall offers ingredients and recipes to inspire shoppers. Admire counters and shelves laden with charcuterie, speciality cheeses, staples, beers and wines, not forgetting the in-house butchery and deli whose staff are on hand to advise.

So be brave, turn off the road to discover Historic England's ruins and much more in this surprising haven of great food and fun.

Creake Abbey

Creake Abbey
NORFOLK PAELLA

This is a Norfolk inspired paella, using wonderful local ingredients including lobster (Cromer crab could be used as an alternative), brown shrimps instead of the usual squid, and samphire rather than green beans. This dish can sometimes be found on our specials board. Perfect for lunch or dinner and great with a cold glass of Chablis. Created in collaboration with Mary Kemp.

Preparation time: 30 minutes | Cooking time: 40 minutes | Serves 6

Ingredients

1 tbsp Norfolk rapeseed oil

250g Marsh Pig Chorizo sausage, chopped

4 skinless Norfolk chicken breasts or boned thighs, chopped

200g cherry tomatoes

4 cloves garlic

1 heaped tsp smoked paprika

100ml dry sherry

600-800ml hot chicken stock

1 red pepper, deseeded and cut into thin strips

1 tsp Norfolk Saffron threads

300g paella rice

200g local brown shrimps

1 Norfolk dressed lobster, chopped into bite sized pieces

200g samphire washed, cleaned woody stalks removed and blanched in hot water

Fresh parsley, chopped

2 lemons, quartered

Method

Grab a large paella or sauté pan and heat up the oil before frying the chorizo, add the chicken and then cook on a gentle heat for about 5 minutes.

While the meat cooks whizz together the tomatoes, garlic, smoked paprika and sherry until smooth, then pass through a sieve to remove the seeds.

Add the tomato sauce to the pan and cook for 10 minutes until the liquid reduces and thickens.

Once you have a rich tomato sauce, pour in 600ml of the chicken stock, add the peppers and saffron and stir together before adding the rice. If the pan gets too dry, add the rest of the stock.

Cook the paella over a gentle heat for a good 20 minutes and try not to stir too much - you should see the rice start to puff up around the meat.

Just before the paella is ready, top the pan with the shrimps, lobster and samphire.

Garnish with chopped parsley and quartered lemons to serve.

A pub
WITH HEART

The Dabbling Duck is a destination dining pub with nine luxurious bedrooms, but it is also a true heart-of-the-community pub where a warm Norfolk welcome is always on offer.

Ten years ago, The Dabbling Duck narrowly escaped being turned into housing when some local farmers got together to take over its running. Its story then took on a new chapter three years ago when Mark Dobby and, shortly after, his wife Sally joined forces with the two remaining farmers Steve and Dom to put The Dabbling Duck firmly on the county's culinary map.

Mark and Sally have an impressive combined history in the hospitality industry, having worked together at Titchwell Manor along with various other award-winning Norfolk restaurants and pubs. Even though Great Massingham isn't a great distance from the coast, Mark and Sally were hugely influenced by their countryside location.

"We are so lucky to have such amazing local produce all around us," enthuses Sally. "The local farmers who supply our meat and the game-keepers who supply our game are regulars in the pub, so when someone asks about where the meat has come from, we can often point the farmer out!"

Head chef Dale Smith has embraced the incredible local produce which often comes directly from the farm to the kitchen door – he continues to smile even when 100 pheasants turn up in the kitchen to be plucked on a Saturday morning! He prepares seasonal ingredients with care and cooks them with creativity. From crab, cockles and shrimps from the coast to venison, woodcock or the amazing Dexter beef from nearby, the seasons dictate what ends up on Dale's menu.

People who come to stay in one of the nine bedrooms often comment on the atmosphere of the bustling pub, and Sally never tires of giving visitors to the county a taste of Norfolk hospitality: "The friendliness and character of the place was what drew us here in the first place. We love the community feel and are so lucky that people support the pub so much."

The ambitious team at The Dabbling Duck are always on the look-out for new ways to push things forward, and in 2016 they added a wood-fired pizza oven to the mix. With plans for a new outdoor bar underway for summer 2017, the garden will be the perfect spot to enjoy a pizza and a beer all summer long.

The Dabbling Duck
MASSINGHAM DEXTER SIRLOIN

We serve the Dexter sirloin with a smoked jus that is cooked for 24 hours, so you will need to start making the jus the day before.

Preparation time: 1 hour | Cooking time: 24 hours | Serves 2

Ingredients

For the smoked jus:
1kg beef bones

1 of each leek, onion, celery stick and carrot

Redcurrant Jelly

400ml red wine, to taste

Smoke oil or powder

For the sirloin:
5g Marmite

20ml vegetable oil

2 x 185g sirloin steaks

For the onion ash:
1 onion

1 leek tops

For the leek purée:
2 white leeks

2 tsp squid ink

2 tsp miso paste

Dash of soy sauce

For the carrot purée:
2 orange carrots

1 vanilla pod

20g butter

1 tsp honey

100ml beef stock

For the carrot fondant:
2 purple heritage carrots

2 yellow heritage carrots

50g butter

2 garlic cloves

10g thyme

50ml beef stock

To serve:
Charred leeks

Carrot crisps

Method

For the smoked jus
Roast 1kg bones in a hot oven until coloured. Roughly cut up a leek, onion, celery stick and carrot, and colour off in a hot pan. Place the vegetables and bones in a deep pan, cover with cold water and place on a low heat. Do not boil. Leave on for 24 hours. Skim the fat off of the stock, and when the stock is ready pass through a sieve. Place the stock into another pan, add redcurrant jelly and red wine, then put on a high heat. Reduce until thick enough to coat the back of a spoon. Season and add some smoke oil or powder to taste.

For the sirloin
Mix the marmite and vegetable oil together and then marinate the meat. Set aside.

For the onion ash
Peel and roughly chop the onion. Break up the leak tops and leave in a hot oven till blackened. Blitz to a powder. You will need 10g of the onion ash.

For the leek purée
Cut the leeks in half lengthways and wash. Blacken both ways on a griddle, then slice and place in a pan. Add 200ml water, bring to the boil and simmer until most of the liquid has reduced. Transfer to a food processor and blitz with the rest of the ingredients. Pass through a sieve.

For the carrot purée
Peel and slice the carrots and place in a pan. Cover with oil and cook over a medium heat until the carrots are soft then blitz with the rest of the ingredients and seasoning. Pass through a sieve.

For the carrot fondants
Preheat the oven to 180°c. Peel the carrots and cut into large rectangles, then colour in a pan on each side. Add the rest of the ingredients and seasoning, and place in the oven until the carrots are cooked through.

For the charred leeks and carrot crisps
Top and tail 6 baby leeks, and colour them on the griddle. Place on a tray with 50g butter and seasoning. Finish in the oven. Shave an orange and heritage yellow carrot until you have shaved about ten crisps off. Heat some oil for deep-frying up to 170°c. Cook the carrot shavings until golden brown then place on kitchen paper and season.

To serve
Cook the steaks to your liking and serve with the onion ash, leek purée, carrot purée, carrot fondant, charred leeks, carrot crisps and smoked jus.

In the SWIM

Global flavours, the best of local produce, and a warm welcome await at The Duck Inn; Stanhoe's award-winning pub restaurant...

In a crowded marketplace, it's a rare Gastropub that stands out from the competition. A stylish, welcoming venue in rural Stanhoe, however, The Duck Inn seems to do it effortlessly. Included in 2017's Michelin Guide, The Duck won 2017's Good Food Guide Restaurant of the Year for the East of England, was awarded the 'One to Watch' in the Morning Advertiser's Top 50 Gastropubs 2017, was listed in Condé Nast's 'Top Five Norfolk Foodie Hotspots', and has been a finalist three years running in the Observer Food Awards 'Best Sunday Roast' Category. It's an impressive haul, but like it's namesake a lot of hard work goes on below the surface of this duck to make the magic happen...

Since launching in 2013, The Duck Inn's success has been built around teamwork, passion, and commitment. Chef patron Ben Handley's twenty-five years behind the stove may have led to The Duck's beautiful balance between adventurous flavours and local, seasonal produce. Ben is ably supported by his wife Sarah, brother, Sam, and a front-of-house and kitchen team with a formidable amount of combined experience.

Their passion and commitment comes across in the food. Everything is kept fresh and as seasonal as possible, with an emphasis on using the best locally sourced produce at all times and then presenting it in exquisitely inventive ways. Whether it's a bowl of Norfolk mussels, meat reared on local farms, or vegetables picked just a few fields away, The Duck Inn provides inspired cooking of the highest order. There is a fine dining experience here, sure, but it's honest and hearty too. Great food with an imaginative twist, if you will.

It isn't just the critics who agree. The Duck Inn has become a firm favourite with loyal customers returning to sample more of its ever-changing delights along with regular signature dishes. For those of us who like nothing more than curling up after a good meal, it offers two elegant rooms, so there's always the option to make a night of it too...

The Duck Inn
VENISON PASTRAMI

This dish came about as we looked for other ways to use this incredible local ingredient and enhance its unique flavour.

Preparation time: 5 days | Cooking time: 5 hours | Serves 4

Ingredients

1 haunch of venison (ask your butcher to tunnel bone and cut into sections for pastrami. At The Duck Inn we use local venison from the nearby Holkham Estate)

For the brine:

4 litres water

400g salt

200g caster sugar

25g pickling spice (we use an all-spice blend, containing coriander seed, juniper, dried chilli, mustard, cloves, peppercorns, and fennel)

3 garlic cloves

2 fresh bay leaves

For the spice rub:

1 tbsp rapeseed oil

3 tbsp black pepper, cracked

2 cloves garlic, crushed

2 tbsp coriander seeds

1 tbsp smoked paprika

1 tbsp fennel seeds

1 tsp dried chilli flakes

1 tsp cumin seeds

To serve:

Pickled vegetables

Rye bread

Mustard

Norfolk Dapple cheese crackers

Method

Placing in a suitable pan, bring all of the brine ingredients to a rolling boil before allowing to cool. When the brine is cold, submerge the venison sections, cover and keep refrigerated for 5 days.

After 5 days remove the venison from the brine and pat dry with kitchen paper.

Preheat the oven to 100°c

Reserving the rapeseed oil, mix the remaining ingredients for the spice rub together, making sure that they are evenly distributed. Massage the spice rub onto the venison. Heat a heavy roasting pan containing the rapeseed oil and brown the venison sections evenly all over.

Placing the venison into a suitable tray, place into the preheated oven and gently cook for 4½ hours.

Remove from the oven and leave to cool. Once cool, wrap tightly in cling film and refrigerate until ready to use.

To serve

At The Duck Inn we serve our venison pastrami with pickled vegetables, rye bread and mustard, finished with Norfolk Dapple cheese crackers.

The Duck Inn
PAN-ROASTED SKATE WING WITH BRANCASTER SHELLFISH BUTTER

In this stunning celebration of the Norfolk coast local, sustainable North Sea fish is paired beautifully with local shellfish and finished with herbs we forage ourselves on the saltmarsh. What's not to like?!

Preparation time: 1 day | Cooking time: 20 minutes | Serves 4

Ingredients

For the skate wing:

2 x 500g skate wing, skinned

For the dry brine:

200g table salt

70g caster sugar

1 lemon, zest

½ tsp fennel seeds

¼ tsp ground white pepper

For the shellfish butter:

1 large banana shallot, finely chopped

1 fennel bulb, finely chopped

150g unsalted butter, cubed

1 tbsp extra virgin olive oil

175ml dry white wine

50ml dry vermouth

To serve:

20 live mussels, scrubbed and rinsed

28 live cockles, rinsed

200g brown shrimps, peeled (optional)

12 spring onions, trimmed

50g sea purslane (if available)

1 tbsp chives, chopped

1 tbsp dill, chopped

1 lemon, juiced

Method

Mix together the dry brine ingredients and allow to infuse for one whole day.

With a pair of scissors, trim around the frilly skirt edge of the skate wings before using a heavy, sharp chef's knife to cut each wing straight down the middle, creating four equal-sized portions. Completely cover all four wings with the dry brine mixture and leave for 8 minutes. After 8 minutes, immediately rinse the skate under cold water, removing all of the brine mixture, before patting dry with kitchen paper.

Transfer the skate wings to the refrigerator until ready to cook.

For the shellfish butter

In a heavy-bottomed saucepan, warm the olive oil and gently sweat the fennel and shallot without colouring. When softened add the wine and vermouth and increase the heat until the liquid has reduced by around two-thirds.

Turn the heat down to low and whisk in the butter until it has melted. Set aside.

To assemble and serve

Placing the skate wings on buttered, greaseproof paper, gently pan-roast in a sauté pan on a medium heat for 5 minutes or until golden brown. Turn the skate over and reduce the heat.

Squeeze over the juice from half a lemon and leave to rest in a warm place until ready to serve.

Warm the infused butter, wine and fennel mix and add the spring onions, mussels and cockles. When the shellfish are all open, add the chopped herbs and optional brown shrimps.

Arrange the skate between four large bowls and divide the shellfish broth between them.

Garnish with fresh sea purslane and serve.

The Duck Inn

ROSARY ASH GOAT'S CHEESE WITH HONEY, PISTACHIO AND DIGESTIVE

We use fabulous ash-rolled goat's cheese from Rosary Creamery, but you could use a local cheese of your choosing. We also make our own quince jelly to lift the dish, but again, beautiful jellies are available to buy following the quince season.

Preparation time: 30 minutes | Cooking time: 30 minutes | Serves 4

Ingredients

For the digestive biscuits:

300g wholemeal flour

100g plain flour

100g fine oatmeal

200g cold butter, diced

120ml milk

100g light brown sugar

2 teaspoon baking powder

1 pinch salt

For the pistachio:

160g pistachio compound

80g pistachios

65g feuilletine

40g icing sugar

4g sea salt

To serve:

400g goat's cheese

Quince jelly

Drizzle of Norfolk honey

Method

To make the digestive biscuits

Preheat the oven to at 180°c.

Mix all the dry ingredients in a mixing bowl until well incorporated.

Add the butter and, using the 'K' beater or paddle beater on a slow setting, beat until it is a breadcrumb-like consistency. Keeping the mixer on, add the milk until mixed thoroughly.

Roll the mixture tightly in cling film into a thick, sausage-like shape and chill.

Once chilled, slice thinly and bake at 180°c for 6 minutes on each side. Cool and store in an airtight container until ready to use.

To make the pistachio

Preheat the oven to at 170°c.

Toast pistachios for 10-15 minutes until golden.

Allow to cool and smash slightly using a rolling pin, or any weapon of your choosing!

Place all ingredients into a bowl and work together until you get varying sized clusters.

To serve

To complete the dish, plate up the pistachio mix, goat's cheese and quince jelly, before adding a couple of delicious digestive biscuits. Finish with a drizzle of Norfolk honey and enjoy.

Forgotten FRUITS

A combined love for growing, making and cooking is behind the story of the extraordinary Norfolk medlar fruit preserves from Eastgate Larder.

Today Jane Steward has one of the more unusual job titles in the country. A medlar farmer, she grows this ancient fruit and produces preserves from her Norfolk home. Once a popular fruit in English gardens, medlars fell out of favour in the 20th century as more fashionable produce arrived in the country.

For Jane, founder of Eastgate Larder, the story began with a single medlar tree growing in her husband's Cambridgeshire garden. Intrigued by its mysterious crop, she trawled recipe books seeking inspiration for what to do with these unfamiliar ingredients. With very little information available, she began experimenting herself, with many disastrous attempts at first. Jane's fascination with the fruit led her on a journey of recipe exploration and development.

When she and her husband moved to Norfolk, the tree came with them, and Jane planted a few more alongside. It was during this time that Jane had a health scare, which totally transformed her outlook on life. Thanks to NHS screening, she was fortunate to be cured of an early-stage cancer. Throughout this time, she took refuge in her garden and kitchen and she found a love for growing and making that excited her so much more than her career.

Full of renewed focus and zest for life, Jane said goodbye to her leadership coaching business and threw herself wholeheartedly into planting, growing and harvesting medlar trees and creating her own hand-made preserves. The business took off much more quickly than she expected and thanks to other Norfolk gardeners she's able to harvest enough fruit to fulfil demand while her orchard matures.

The new connections made within the food community have deepened her commitment to Norfolk and Jane is well known for her passion for the county. She explains how the distinctive flavour of the medlar works so well with local produce, from paté and game to roast and cold meats and cheeses. It can be stirred into sauces or even spread on toast.

With 100 trees now on the site, Eastgate Larder is a medlar specialist. Jane chooses not to work with any other produce so that she can focus her full attention on this remarkable fruit. She has lots of ideas for exciting future products... the possibility of a medlar gin is just one of those intriguing prospects!

Eastgate Larder

BAKED APPLES WITH SPICED MEDLAR CHEESE

A new twist on baked apples. These are delicious served with fresh custard, vanilla ice cream, cream or Greek yoghurt.

Preparation time: 20 minutes | Cooking time: 20 minutes | Serves 4

Ingredients

1 x 100g jar Eastgate Larder Medlar Cheese

40g raisins or sultanas

20g walnuts, chopped

Small pinch of ground cloves

½ tsp ground cinnamon

4 medium Bramley apples, cored and unpeeled

Method

Preheat oven to 180°c. Mix together the Eastgate Larder Medlar Cheese, dried fruit, chopped walnuts, ground cloves and cinnamon. Pack the mixture into the cavity of each apple. Score each apple at its widest point and place on a lined baking sheet. Bake in the preheated oven for 20 minutes. Allow to cool slightly before serving.

PHEASANT BREASTS WITH THYME AND MEDLAR JELLY

Delicious served with oven roasted beetroot, parsnips or carrots and finely shredded steamed Savoy cabbage.

Preparation time: 20 minutes | Cooking time: 20 minutes | Serves 4

Ingredients

50g butter, plus extra if needed

1 tbsp olive oil, plus extra if needed

2 red onions, finely sliced

5 sprigs of thyme

1 dessert apple, unpeeled and sliced

4 skinless pheasant breasts

2 tbsp Eastgate Larder Medlar Jelly

100ml dry sherry

Salt and pepper

Method

Melt 25g of the butter and the olive oil in a shallow pan and add the sliced onions and thyme. Fry gently until the onion is caramelised. Remove to a plate. Melt the remaining 25g of the butter in the pan, add the apple slices and turn gently until they are golden. Remove to a plate.

Season the pheasant breasts with salt and pepper. Cook in the same pan, adding a little more oil and butter if necessary, turning the breasts to get a good colour. After 5 minutes, add the sherry and the Eastgate Larder Medlar Jelly. Increase the heat until the sherry and jelly are bubbling. Add the caramelised onions and the apple slices to the pan and reduce the heat. Check the seasoning and serve.

Creme de LA CRÉME

Where pre-theatre pick-me-ups shine and first dates don't have to end, Figbar is a contemporary dessert bar that will amplify your sweet tooth.

Figbar is the brainchild of husband-and-wife team Jaime and Stephanie Garbutt. They first met in Norwich in 2007 when Tennessee-born Stephanie was completing her MA in Creative Writing before pastry chef Jaime wooed her with a whirlwind tour of Norfolk's established culinary scene. They miraculously had the business up and running within 6 weeks with some dubious help from their first daughter Ella and this was while Stephanie was heavily pregnant with newest Figbar family member Ariele.

Let's start by saying that this is not your typical crêpes, waffles and ice cream sundaes dessert parlour, this is a place that brings Michelin-style plated desserts into focus. The menu is curated by executive pastry chef Jaime who has featured on numerous international media programmes, opened restaurants in London and Hong Kong and has worked with the likes of Marcus Wareing, Gordon Ramsay, Galton Blackiston, Yotam Ottolenghi and Richard Bainbridge.

Each day the counter is filled with freshly made cakes, financiers and exquisite sweet treats that vary daily. They also run a premium dessert menu of five which vary based on season and inspiration. Jaffa cakes, chocolate bundt cake, banana buckeye cake, PB&J financier, twice-baked chocolate torte, cherry bakewell, and freshly ground coffee are just a few of the delights you might find upon entering Figbar. One of their most popular desserts, Snickers, features on several of Jaime's menus around the world – peanut butter parfait, chocolate mousse, caramel sauce, powdered Nutella and peanut praline, a nostalgia-inducing classic which you can see being concocted in their open kitchen.

"Very few places offer what we do. The culture in England is to go out and drink at night but that isn't everyone's cup of tea. We are a late night place for people to go to that isn't a pub," says Jaime. If you do fancy making a night of it, the atmosphere comes alive in the evening with great music and your tipple of choice - choose from wine, Champagne or perhaps a dessert wine to pair with your pudding.

The intimate venue only seats 20 so you'll have to fight the regulars for a seat, some people sit in all day and work through the entire dessert menu! Figbar is not meant to be a one trick pony so this dynamic duo is definitely one to watch…

Figbar

Figbar
POPCORN GONE BANANAS

Chef Jaime Garbutt first conceived this plated dessert while head of pastry at the Playboy Club in London, Mayfair, for their infamous Midsummer Party. It is a playful throwback to cinema date nights coupled with the familiarity of sweet banana bread. Make sure the bananas are very ripe – the blacker the better – and you'll get the sweet gooey texture you're after.

Preparation time: 3 hours| Chill time: 2 hours | Serves 4-6

Ingredients

For the popcorn ice cream:

2 x 70g bags of butter microwave popcorn, popped

¼ tsp table salt

500g double cream

500g whole milk

215g egg yolks

100g caster sugar

70g glucose

For the banana financier:

62g butter

100g caster sugar

2 bananas, very ripe

85g egg whites

45g plain flour

62g ground almonds

For the banana caramel jelly:

100g caster sugar

1 banana, very ripe, mashed

½ lime, juiced

40g crème de bananes

1 gelatine leaf

75g crème fraîche

For the banana caramel sauce:

90g caster sugar

60g glucose

1 banana, very ripe, mashed

25ml Crème de Bananes

25g double cream

Pinch of salt

For the popcorn hazelnut praline:

125g caster sugar

30g salted butter

20g popped popcorn

40g hazelnuts, chopped

Method

For the ice cream

Cover the popcorn with milk in a medium saucepan. Bring to the boil, remove from the heat and cool completely. Pour into a blender with the salt and cream and blitz for 30 seconds. Pass the mixture through a fine sieve into a bowl and top with enough milk to reach 700g. Place yolks, sugar, and glucose into a large bowl and set aside. Return the popcorn milk mixture to saucepan and bring to the boil. Pour this over the egg yolk mix. Return the combination to the saucepan and whisk constantly over a medium heat until it reaches 84°c. Remove, pass through a sieve and allow to cool. Churn the mixture in an ice cream machine.

For the banana financier

Preheat your fan-assisted oven to 165°c and then start making a beurre noisette by melting the butter in a pan over a medium heat. Turn up the heat and boil the butter until it stops bubbling and turns a golden brown nutty colour. Remove from the heat and set aside. In a large bowl using a wooden spoon, beat the remaining ingredients together until smooth. Slowly add the beurre noisette and beat until well combined. Pour into a mini muffin tray and place in the oven for 10 minutes until golden. De-mould and allow to cool.

For the banana caramel jelly

Heat the sugar in a medium saucepan stirring constantly until light golden brown. Add mashed bananas and stir until the caramel is darker and very thick. Add the lime juice and crème de bananes and cook until thick and sticky. Remove from the heat and allow the bubbling to stop. Add gelatine and mix until dissolved before stirring in the crème fraîche. Pass through a sieve and chill in the fridge for at least 2 hours.

For the banana caramel sauce

Heat the sugar, glucose and one tablespoon of water in a saucepan over a medium heat stirring constantly until it reaches a dark colour. Add the banana and continue stirring until it breaks down into a thick dark paste. Add the Crème de Bananes and mix. Remove from the heat; add the cream and a pinch of salt and then mix with a hand blender. Pass through sieve and chill in the fridge for least 2 hours.

For the popcorn hazelnut praline

Heat the sugar over a medium heat to a light caramel. Whisk in the butter to emulsify before adding the popcorn and hazelnuts, fold until completely coated. Pour onto a cold surface and break apart as it cools.

To serve

Spoon a heaped teaspoon of caramel onto a plate and smear across with the back of a spoon. Arrange three warm financiers along the smear followed by three cut spoonfuls of jelly. Scatter with broken praline. Finally, nestle a scoop of ice cream in the centre. Serve immediately.

Galton Blackiston

PAN-FRIED WILD SEA BASS WITH SQUID RISOTTO AND NERO SAUCE

Galton Blackiston at Morston Hall has retained a Michelin star for an unprecedented 18th successive year, as well as being awarded four AA rosettes. Chef patron Galton said: "We're absolutely thrilled to have retained our Michelin star, which means we've held the honour for every year since our first award back in 1999. We believe that's an unprecedented achievement for any restaurant in this part of the country."

This striking dish is made with the freshest sea bass and squid, which is combined with salsify to make a delicious and simple risotto base.

Preparation time: 10 minutes | Cooking time: 20 minutes | Serves 2

Ingredients

4 sticks of salsify, peeled and cooked

150g squid, roughly chopped

Splash of lemon juice

1 teaspoon pickled ginger

2 x 175g fillets of sea bass, de-scaled

2 tbsp rapeseed oil

Butter, for cooking

Salt and pepper

Nero sauce, to serve

Method

Purée three of the sticks of cooked salsify in a food processor or blender. Cook the squid and add to the purée and season, then warm through, adding a splash of lemon juice and add a teaspoon of pickled sushi ginger.

Fry the remaining salsify in butter and season well.

Pan-fry the sea bass in the rapeseed oil. Serve the sea bass on the squid risotto and place the pan-fried salsify alongside. Serve with nero sauce.

Galton Blackiston at Morston Hall

morstonhall
HOTEL & RESTAURANT

Holy MOLY

The Cathedral of St John the Baptist is a catholic church that welcomes people from all walks of life to visit and taste the delights that The Garden Café has to offer.

When you picture Victorian Gothic revival Cathedrals, cafés aren't usually the first thing that springs to mind. In 2010, after years of fundraising, the church received a lottery grant and the Narthex building, including a café and gift shop, opened its doors. It has been a welcome addition to the grand place of worship and since then many people have visited to enjoy a bite to eat in the stunning gardens.

Plans for the Cathedral itself commenced in the 1870s, but it wasn't completed until 1910 after years of intricate design and building work. The hard work paid off and resulted in a stunning piece of architecture that is now a Grade I - listed building of exceptional interest. Duke Henry Fitzalan Howard funded the creation, as thanks for his first marriage to Lady Flora Abney-Hastings. It was a gift to the Catholics and today it is one of Norwich's most iconic buildings with thousands of visitors and around 1200 regular worshippers.

The café offers wholesome breakfasts, fresh sandwiches, warming soups and traditional small plates. If you have a sweet tooth, then you are in luck with afternoon tea and homemade cakes sold to satisfy any cravings. From plot to plate, all the food served is locally sourced to create the freshest of dishes. "We like to utilise the garden surroundings and bring the garden into the café, during the summer months the vegetables and fruits come from our allotments and gardens at the Cathedral and the Bishop's house," says general manager Gavin Wood who, along with his new catering supervisor Kate Wakefield, is hoping to up the ante with the menu in the upcoming months.

Various different components make up the Narthex and each room oozes character. The Duke Henry suite is an ideal room for a wedding or celebration and Mac's bar is a fully licensed bar and ideal for small functions and conferences. The Perowne Room, which is airy and bright, leads on to the wonderful gardens right in the heart of the city, that are unknown to many. Great credit for the gardens must go to the head gardener Zanna Foley–Davies and her team of volunteers.

The venue has a real sense of community which has made the Cathedral more accessible to all kinds of people, volunteers work hard in all areas to make it a pleasant place to visit and to welcome everyone with open arms.

The Garden Café
THE CATHEDRAL OF ST JOHN
THE BAPTIST HOT CROSS BUNS

On Tuesday of Holy Week, the Bishop, joined by the priests of the Diocese, gather at the Cathedral to celebrate the Chrism Mass. This tradition manifests the unity of the priests with their Bishop. We always celebrate the end of the mass for around 1000 people with refreshments and our hot cross buns.

Preparation time: 15 minutes | Proving time: 90 minutes | Cooking time: 12-14 minutes | Serves 8

Ingredients

For the dough:

25g fresh yeast

25g sugar

60ml warm water

300g strong bread flour

2 tsp ground cinnamon

2 tsp mixed spice

30g butter

125ml warm milk

75g mixed fruit

1 egg

For the flour paste:

37g plain flour

½ tbsp caster sugar

40ml water

For the glaze:

45ml milk

25g caster sugar

Method

First mix the yeast with the sugar and the warm water.

Then place the flour, cinnamon and mixed spice into a bowl before rubbing in the butter.

Add the egg, dried fruit, yeast mixture and milk – bring everything together to form a sticky dough and knead for 10 minutes.

Leave in a greased bowl covered with cling film and leave to rise for 1 hour.

Knock back the dough after 1 hour and divide into 8 evenly sized buns and place on a baking tray lined with parchment paper.

Leave to prove in a warm place for a further 30 minutes until they have doubled in size, meanwhile preheat the oven to 200°c.

Mix up the ingredients for the flour paste and place in piping bag. Once the buns have finished proving, pipe a cross on each bun.

Bake the buns for 12–14 minutes. To check if cooked, turn over a bun and pat the base – you should hear a hollow sound.

To make the glaze, heat up the milk and caster sugar together then brush the mixture over the top of the warm buns.

Goodies from THE GARDEN

For preserve-makers The Garden Pantry, their own garden and the natural Norfolk larder provide all the ingredients needed for their all-natural hand-made jams and chutneys.

The Garden Pantry are based in Spooner Row in the heart of Norfolk, where Neil Griffin and Becky Slater grow a variety of fruit and vegetables which they then transform into a whole host of jams, marmalades, chutneys, sauces and pickles.

It often comes as a surprise that such a diverse range of preserves – they currently produce over 50 products – are all made by hand by Becky and Neil from their Norfolk home. Watching fruit and vegetables grow from scratch is what makes the process so special for the green-fingered pair, as they really can boast a seed-to-jar journey for their ingredients. Anything that they can't grow themselves is sourced locally.

The Garden Pantry began life when Neil and Becky made a batch of courgette chutney from a glut of courgettes in their garden. Today the huge range is famous for some unusual flavours, such as their irresistible cocktail range – think Blackberry and Gin Jam, Raspberry and Amaretto Jam or Rhubarb and prosecco Jam. The alcohol can certainly be tasted, too! The Strawberry Daiquiri Jam came highly commended in the Great British Food Awards 2016.

For a truly local flavour, the Spiced Bean Chutney is a must-try. Made with runner beans from the garden and Norfolk's own Colman's mustard power, it won a Great Taste Gold Star in 2013. They have since accrued more Great Taste awards in 2014, 2015 and 2016 by developing delicious preserves that stand out from the usual offerings. With awards stacking up, they were overwhelmed to be selected by Theo Phaphitis as a winner of Small Business Sunday in 2016.

As well as the interesting flavour combinations, Neil and Becky put their success down to the quality of the produce in the jars. All of the jams have high fruit content, with a minimum of 50% fruit. They have also gained a loyal following because every single product is totally gluten-free.

Although they maintain a core range, they also produce some limited edition, seasonal products, which depend on each year's harvest. As a small artisan maker, they have the flexibility to respond to the seasons and produce some deliciously different preserves that reflect what is growing around them.

The Garden Pantry
BRIOCHE PUDDING

An alternative to the classic bread and butter pudding, this simple dish is quick and easy to prepare and tastes great. It's a great way to use up some leftover brioche loaf or you could even use croissants. We like to use our fresh duck eggs in this pudding which adds to the richness of the flavours. As an alternative to the Rhubarb and Orange Marmalade why not try The Garden Pantry's Rhubarb and prosecco Jam, delicious!

Preparation time: 10 minutes | Cooking time: 40 minutes | Serves 4

Ingredients

8 slices of brioche butter loaf

3 tbsp Rhubarb and Orange Marmalade from The Garden Pantry

3 medium eggs

285ml semi-skimmed milk

1 tbsp sugar

Butter, to grease the dish

Custard, cream or ice cream, to serve

Method

Preheat the oven to 180°c (gas 4). Lightly grease an 18cm Pyrex dish (or suitable alternative) with butter.

Generously spread the marmalade over four slices of the brioche loaf. Cut all eight slices of the brioche into quarters and proceed to lay the slices over the base of the dish, alternating layers of the marmalade-covered squares and plain squares, with the last layer being plain (to avoid the marmalade burning on the top).

Whisk the eggs, milk and sugar together and pour over the brioche. Use a fork to press down gently to ensure all the bread has absorbed some of the mixture. Cook for 35-40 minutes until golden brown on top and cooked through.

Serve warm with custard, fresh single cream or ice cream.

Ticks all the BOXES

The Georgian Townhouse is a hidden city oasis where you can come to escape the hustle and bustle of everyday life.

Combining Georgian interior design with an excellent location, locally sourced quality produce, evolving seasonal menus, 22 boutique bedrooms and an extensive selection of craft beers, wines and spirits, The Georgian Townhouse ticks all the right boxes and is one of Norwich's best kept secrets - until now.

Picture high ceilings, huge windows, original vintage pieces and an enormous walled garden which stretches all the way down to some lovely stable blocks at the bottom. It's no wonder this impressive al fresco dining spot won them first place in the Norwich in Bloom competition for 'commercial premises'.

Their daily menu presents a varied selection of food to suit every occasion, seasonally created by their passionate kitchen team who take inspiration from local produce wherever possible. You have your simple and approachable dishes like fish and chips, burgers and spit-roast chicken as well as some à la carte dishes if you feel like pushing the boat out. The local butchers down the road, Spurgeons, supply their sausages, Norfolk charcuterie comes from Marsh Pig and they get their fish from Howard & Son. There's also a focus on vegan, vegetarian and gluten-free options - this is a place for folks from all walks of life.

Along with a strong list of gins, they have six rotating hand pulls which host a great selection of firm favourites and limited edition kegs from neighbouring breweries in and around Norwich including St Andrews Brewhouse, Adnams, Grain, Woodfordes & Humpty Dumpty. Attend one of their wine tastings to explore their eclectic mix of old and new world, organic and natural. Or perhaps one of their other regular in-house events is more up your street such as dining at their annual 'Mussel Mania' extravaganza or attending their Summer Garden Party with live music, BBQ, cocktails and a range of their suppliers on hand, showcasing their wares!

With an adjoining bar, private garden and fantastic array of private dining options, their 'Pembroke Rooms', 'Scout Hut' and stables areas are perfect for private event hire whether it's for a formal dinner, conference or maybe a summer barbecue party.

"We like to think that whatever you fancy, we've got it covered! Whether it be a quick pint or coffee, somewhere to bring the family, a slap-up dinner or a relaxed meeting place. We'll make sure you leave well fed and watered one way or another!" says General Manager, Luke Curry.

The Georgian Townhouse
WEST NORFOLK HERITAGE CARROT AND PEARL BARLEY 'RISOTTO'

Our heritage carrot and pearl barley 'risotto' is something a little different and demonstrates, not only our passion for local produce, but also our desire to ensure we have something for everyone. The guinea fowl can be replaced with a host of alternatives, a crispy skinned pan-fried salmon or sea bass fillet would work beautifully, particularly with the presence of the fennel pesto which matches up so well with fish!

Preparation time: 30 minutes | Cooking time: 90 minutes | Serves 6

Ingredients

500g heritage carrots

1 carton of orange juice

Pinch of sugar

750g pearl barley

2 tbsp olive oil

1 litre of good quality vegetable stock

6 guinea fowl breasts, skin on

Butter, for cooking with

100g Roquito chilli pepper pearls

1 head of red chicory

Pea shoots, to garnish

For the carrot ketchup:

500g carrots, roughly chopped

400ml white wine vinegar

200ml water

300g caster sugar

1 tsp ground star anise

½ tsp ginger

1 tsp onion powder

4 garlic cloves

Salt and pepper

For the fennel pesto:

1 bulb of fennel, roughly chopped

100g pine nuts

100g Parmesan cheese, grated

Olive oil

Salt and pepper

Method

For the carrot ketchup

Place all ingredients into a large pan and cook until tender; this will probably take around 25 minutes. Once cooked, blend with a blender or hand mixer into a smooth purée.

For the fennel pesto

Preheat the oven to 140°c.

Slowly roast the chopped fennel for 45 minutes until soft. Then blend with the remaining ingredients until a pesto consistency is formed.

For the 'risotto'

Top and tail the heritage carrots and cut into desired shape. We prefer batons, we also prefer not to peel the carrots as you lose so much flavour, a good wash should suffice.

Cook the carrots in orange juice with salt and pepper and a pinch of sugar until the carrots are just cooked. Allow them to cool in the orange juice and set aside for later.

Empty the pearl barley into a large pan with the olive oil. Allow this to toast for 2-3 minutes, stirring to ensure this does not burn on the bottom. Slowly add half of the vegetable stock, bringing it to the boil. Cook on a medium heat, stirring every 2-3 minutes.

Preheat the oven to 180°c.

With your 'risotto' underway, season and roast the guinea fowl in a hot pan with butter and olive oil, skin side down for 5-6 minutes until the skin is turning a golden brown. Take off the heat and pop in the oven for 5-6 minutes to finish.

Whilst your guinea fowl is cooking, continue to add more stock to your risotto as required, until the pearl barley is nearly cooked. This should take around 10 minutes; pearl barley should be cooked so that it just holds on a spoon, to the consistency of a risotto. Add the carrot ketchup from earlier and salt and pepper to taste, set aside for later.

Add the heritage carrots to the guinea fowl pan and lightly toss in the butter to add some colour, then allow both to rest together in the pan. Whilst this is resting, take your warm plates and place a teaspoon of the fennel pesto prepared earlier into the centre of the plate, and smear with the back of the spoon.

Add a handful (6-7) of the Roquito chillies around the plate, then scatter the warm heritage carrots over the top. Divide the pearl barley between the plates, almost hiding the carrots/chillies/pesto.

Slice the breasts of guinea fowl at an angle, and place on top of the pearl barley. Garnish with pea shoots and chicory leaves standing in the risotto, and glaze with a good dash of olive oil.

Deliciously HOME-GROWN

For those who like to know the provenance of their food, there is no better place to sample some of Norfolk's best home-grown produce than at Green Pastures – a plant centre and farm shop with an award-winning restaurant to boot.

A family-run plant centre and farm shop, Green Pastures has been proudly independent for 25 years. It has been run by Michelle and James since 2009 when they took over the business from Michelle's parents, and since then they have continued to make sure that Green Pastures remains an intrinsic part of the local community.

In 2015 Green Pastures completed the first phase of an exciting expansion project, building a new garden shop and introducing a restaurant to the site. They can now also boast a post office counter, which cements their role as a community hub and has proved extremely popular.

The Gardener's Kitchen Restaurant is perhaps the jewel in the crown. It is certainly no ordinary garden centre café, it has already become one of the region's stand-out dining destinations having won 'Norfolk's Best Restaurant' in the Norfolk Food Awards.

It opened in May 2015 and was packed with customers from day one. Its identity is shaped by its surroundings amid the plant centre and farm shop. The chefs are lucky enough to get to work with a plethora of home-grown fruits, vegetables, salad leaves and herbs that are fresh from the ground, as well as the bounty of the farm shop which sells some of the area's finest produce.

Over 40 varieties of herbs and salads are grown just outside the doors, including asparagus, squashes, leeks, beetroot, beans, brassicas and rhubarb. Chefs experiment with whatever is picked each day to create super-seasonal dishes – at the height of the season, the salad is a unique celebration of home-grown goodies.

The restaurant has understandably become popular with vegetarians looking to try deliciously different meat-free dishes, but there is lots of top-quality meat on the menu too – the cooked breakfast was praised by the Norwich-based 'Fry-up Inspector'! it is also popular with families thanks to the children's corner, which contains toys to entertain little ones while grown-ups enjoy a bite to eat.

If the restaurant has whetted your appetite, the farm shop is the perfect place to stock up your own kitchen. Over 70 Norfolk and Suffolk growers and businesses keep the shop supplied. James starts his day at 4.30am to select the finest quality goods – so customers can rest assured only the best local produce makes it onto the shelves.

Green Pastures

BINHAM BLUE AND TOMATO QUICHE WITH CHARRED ASPARAGUS AND GOLDEN BEETROOT

A wonderful dish for celebrating Norfolk produce, especially some of our own home-grown favourites! Quiche is a very flexible option so you can vary the ingredients according to what's in season. We've included our favourite cheese, Binham Blue, a soft blue-veined cheese from North Norfolk. Serve with golden beetroot, they don't stain and they're much sweeter than their red counterparts!

Preparation time: 30 minutes, plus 30 minutes chilling | Cooking time: 1 hour | Serves 4

Ingredients

For the pastry:

170g plain flour, plus extra for dusting

Pinch of salt

85g butter, cubed, plus extra for greasing

1 medium egg (free-range of course!)

Water, to bind

For the filling:

200g cherry tomatoes, halved

5 large eggs

150ml milk

250ml double cream

140g Binham Blue cheese, grated

Olive oil, for roasting

Sea salt and pepper

To serve (per portion):

1 golden beetroot, cooked

4 asparagus spears

Poached egg

Salad leaves and chopped herbs

Method

For the pastry

Sift the flour together with a pinch of salt into a mixing bowl. Rub in the butter to create a breadcrumb texture. Gently whisk the egg and mix it in with a little water, if needed, to create a firm dough. Cover with cling film and rest in the fridge for 30 minutes.

Preheat the oven to 160˚c. Lightly grease a standard quiche tin.

Lightly dust your work surface with flour and roll out the pastry into the lightly greased quiche tin. Fill with baking beans and bake blind for 20 minutes, then remove the beans and bake for a further 10 minutes.

For the filling

Meanwhile, roast the halved tomatoes with a little olive oil and sea salt for 10 minutes. Beat together the eggs, milk and cream, then add the grated Binham Blue and roasted tomatoes. Pour the mixture into the pastry base and bake for 35-40 minutes until the filling is set and starting to turn a slightly golden brown.

To serve

While the quiche is baking, bring a pan of water to a simmer, add the golden beetroot and simmer for approximately 45 minutes until soft. Peel while still warm and slice into thin rounds. Set aside. Peel the asparagus, keep the trimmings as these can be used to mix into the salad. Dry the asparagus with a paper towel and chargrill to achieve criss-cross lines. Repeat this with the beetroot.

Serve the quiche, asparagus, beetroot and poached egg with fresh salad leaves and chopped herbs to taste.

Charm, PERIOD

Family-run, The Grove, Cromer, joins all of the dots to create an intimate, sumptuous experience...

You either have charm and character, or you don't. If you don't, well, they aren't things you can buy off the shelf. They're things that develop over time with the right approach. The Grove has both, but then it has something of a head-start. Its origins go back to the mid-eighteenth century with the Barclays of banking fame making it their country retreat in the nineteenth century. The Graveling family have owned the property since the mid-twentieth century, but it's the approach that brothers Chris and Richard are taking in the twenty-first that's really putting the place on the map.

Take the food. Those of us lucky enough to have been served vegetables fresh from the garden or perhaps a fish caught only hours before know that it's a truism that the fresher the food, the greater the taste experience. This approach is a foundation stone of The Grove's menus. Where possible what's presented on the plate comes from its gardens. Their output is supported by the very best Norfolk has to offer – which given the county's reputation means diners experience some of the best produce Britain has to offer. Rare-breed meat and poultry from local farms, for example, award-winning cheeses from nearby dairies, or lobsters caught locally, seasonally, and to order by a long-established fishing family.

The emphasis is on simplicity, but that doesn't mean workaday. The Grove puts the very highest-quality ingredients together in inventive, flavoursome ways – an approach that has won the establishment two AA rosettes. The fresh Cromer lobster with wild garlic and chilli Sauce recipe uses wild garlic from the garden, chillies from the greenhouse, and fresh-caught lobster to stunning effect, for example.

The Grove's delicious dishes are presented in equally exquisite period surroundings. The Green Room, which can be traced back to the original Georgian house, is available for private dining parties while The Study offers an elegant, refined experience. The food served in both springs from the same kitchen, overseen and supported by a formidable team to ensure that the quality and service remains outstanding in each.

In our health-conscious times where every calorie is counted, 'eat, drink, and be merry' has fallen far more out of favour than it should. The Grove believes the two aren't incompatible. Eat well, live well is an ethos at the heart of what it does. With charming cottages and yurts available for visitors and 'glampers' alike, there is no reason not to make a night of it, wake up refreshed the next morning, and perhaps go back for seconds...

The Grove

FRESH CROMER LOBSTER WITH GARLIC AND CHILLI SAUCE AND CROMER CRAB RISOTTO

We like to think that all of our dishes are special here at The Grove, but one of the most popular and certainly the best reviewed from our à la carte menu involves our fabulous Cromer lobster. We order ours directly from John Davies – it's the best way to ensure fantastic flavour. Dressing them yourself might be for the adventurous (go on, give it a go!) but served with wild garlic from our garden and chilli from our greenhouse they're well worth the effort!

Preparation time: 15 minutes | Cooking time: 40 minutes | Serves 4

Ingredients

1 lobster, fresh

For the chilli sauce:

1 red pepper

2 red chilli peppers

100ml white wine vinegar

100g caster sugar

100ml water

For the garlic butter:

100g good quality butter (flavour is key, so use a good quality semi-salted or unsalted butter)

2 cloves of fresh garlic, chopped

For the crab risotto:

2 tbsp olive oil

1 tbsp butter

1 shallot, chopped

4 sprigs of thyme

1 tbsp Worcestershire sauce

1 tsp paprika

350g risotto rice

350g pearl barley

Bunch of parsley, chopped

250ml white wine

750ml vegetable or fish stock, hot

One fresh, dressed crab (Cromer for preference!)

1 lemon, juiced and zest

Method

Preheat oven to 190°c (gas mark five).

For the chilli sauce

Deseed the red pepper and both chilli peppers. Discard seeds.

Place all the ingredients in a pan together, bring to the boil and then simmer gently for 10 minutes until the liquid begins to turn pink. Remove from heat, allow to cool, and then placing the mixture in a food processor and blend until smooth. Return the mixture to the pan and gently cook for 20 minutes until sticky.

For the garlic butter

Take the butter out of the fridge an hour before starting to cook to allow it to soften. Beat the butter with a wooden spoon until it is soft and creamy. Add the chopped garlic, folding it into the butter until it is evenly distributed.

For the lobster

Rinse the lobster under running water. Using a sharp knife, cut the lobster in half lengthways. It will need some force as the shells are tough, so be careful!

Remove anything brownish-grey from the interior and discard. Remove the rest of the tail meat from the shell and put it to one side.

Brush the inside of the shell with chilli sauce and then carefully replace the tail meat. Cracking open the claws, remove the meat and place it with the tail meat inside the split shell. Spread the garlic butter on the lobster and then coat with the remainder of the chilli sauce. Placing it on a tray, place in the preheated oven and bake for 10-15 minutes until piping hot.

For the risotto

Heat the oil and butter in a pan over a low heat. Add the shallot and gently fry for around 5 minutes. Add the thyme, worcestershire sauce and paprika before increasing to a medium heat, add the rice and pearl barley, turning it to coat it in the oil, butter, and shallot before cooking for a few minutes.

Add the wine, and gently stir until absorbed. While stirring, gradually add the stock, allowing each addition to be absorbed by the rice before adding the next.

When the last of the stock is almost absorbed, add the crab meat, and gently fold in, adding the parsley, lemon juice and zest. Season and then remove from the heat. Cover and allow to stand for 5 minutes before serving.

Serve immediately, and eat hot, preferably with fingers!

Bucking the TREND

You just can't beat the best local produce, bursting with flavour, put together with a twist – an approach that the Honingham Buck has made its own. Combine this with a respect for tradition and modern technique and you have food that both comforts and inspires.

Lovingly restored and standing in the heart of the beautiful village of Honingham, yet only minutes from Norwich city centre, the Honingham Buck is an inspired partnership between Tania and Henry Watt, the team behind some of Norfolk's best-loved hostelries, and Lacons Brewery, an award-winning Great Yarmouth brewery with a 250-year heritage.

Traditionalists will enjoy the flexibility offered by a selection of bar nibbles and pub classics whilst the trademark dishes within the main menu satisfy the more adventurous or cosmopolitan guest.

The Buck's partnership with Lacons is a vital ingredient. Lacons rich brewing history and heritage offers quality hand crafted ales modernised to match modern palates. There are always four Lacons ales available featuring their core, heritage, and seasonal ales and of course Encore, voted world's best bitter under 4% in 2015.

Service is at the heart of what the Honingham Buck offers, combining the warmth of old-fashioned hospitality with a dollop of professionalism thrown in. The whole ethos centres around guests being able to leave the frantic pace of today's world behind them. Sitting around a table enjoying good food and drink with friends, family or colleagues is one of life's simplest pleasures. The Buck's team's sole objective is to provide the space, the service and the food that makes that experience happen in the best possible way.

Chocolate-box pretty, and featuring a sympathetically-restored beamed bar, a comfortably stylish restaurant and a large beer-garden perfect for sunny, lazy days, the Honingham Buck also has eight newly-built bed and breakfast rooms. It's the sort of place perfect for leaving the world behind, whether that be for a pint, lunch, dinner, or an overnight stay. Step through the door and give it a try...

The Koningham Buck
LOWESTOFT COD MASALA

Created by head chef Ryan Mace, this recipe has been an instant hit since it was first introduced on our menu. The flavour combinations work beautifully, making it a dish perfect for a special supper or a showstopper to impress friends at a dinner party.

Preparation time: 30 minutes | Cooking time: 20 minutes | Serves 4

Ingredients

For the spice mix:

2 tsp cumin seeds

4 tsp coriander seeds

1 tsp turmeric

½ tsp cayenne pepper

½ tsp black pepper, freshly ground

For the brine mix:

50g sea salt

500ml water

For the sauce:

75g clarified butter

½ onion, peeled and sliced

1 tsp spice mix (see method below)

25g garlic, grated

25g ginger, ginger

1 stick of cinnamon

3 cloves

1 cardamom pod

2 bay leaves

1 ½ tsp fenugreek seeds

250ml fresh fish stock

400ml coconut milk

For the main dish:

½ cauliflower

100g seashore vegetables (such as sea aster, sea beet, sea purslane)

4 x 150g Lowestoft cod loins

200g wild rice

400g chicken or vegetable stock (or water)

80g sprouted chickpeas

Rapeseed oil, for frying

½ lemon, juiced

Seasoning

Method

To make the spice mix

Heat a dry frying pan over a low heat, add the cumin seeds and roast until aromatic, remove from the pan and set aside, repeat with the coriander seeds. Putting the seeds in a blender, blitz the seeds to a fine powder before mixing in the turmeric, cayenne and freshly ground black pepper, store in an airtight Kilner jar to maintain freshness.

To make the brine

Place the sea salt and water into a pan and bring to the boil, once boiled, remove from heat, allow it to cool, place in the fridge to chill.

To make the sauce

Place clarified butter in a saucepan and bring to temperature over a medium heat, add sliced onion and sauté until well browned, but not burnt, stirring frequently, when they start to colour add the fenugreek seeds.

Next add the grated garlic and ginger together with the cinnamon, cloves, cardamom and bay leaves, continue to stir throughout, when the onions are well browned, reduce the heat and add 1 tsp of the spice mix from earlier and continue to cook for a couple of minutes.

Next add the fish stock, turn up the heat a little and simmer to reduce by one quarter, add the coconut milk and continue to simmer and reduce until the desired thickness is achieved (the sauce should coat the back of a spoon). Remove from the heat, strain through a j-cloth or muslin into a bowl, push cling film down onto the sauce to prevent a skin forming before setting aside and leaving to cool.

To cook and serve the fish

Cut the cauliflower into individual florets, pick, wash and dry the sea vegetables, set both aside, place the cod and cauliflower into a bowl, cover with the brine solution and leave for 6 minutes. After 6 minutes remove from the brine, drain thoroughly, pat dry with kitchen paper and set aside on a j-cloth, place the rice and stock into a pan and bring to the boil over a medium heat, cook for 10-15 minutes until al dente.

Meanwhile, place the sauce and chickpeas into a saucepan and bring up to temperature over a low heat, taste and season, heating a large non-stick frying pan over a medium heat, lightly coat the base with rapeseed oil. When the pan is hot, add the cod skin side down and cook for 4-5 minutes, while the cod is cooking, heat another large non-stick pan over a medium heat and add oil.

Add the cauliflower florets and sauté until golden before adding the sea vegetables and cooking for a further minute, seasoning with lemon juice to taste. Remove and set aside on j-cloth, turn the cod over and then remove from the heat before allowing to rest for 1 minute. Drain the rice. Place a piece of cod into the centre of a warmed serving plate with the rice, cauliflower and sea vegetables around it. Spoon around plenty of the warmed sauce and serve immediately.

The Connoisseur's CHOICE

Multi award-winning Lakenham Creamery have been making quality ice cream in Norwich since 1921.

Lakenham Creamery was founded by a gentleman called Christmas Aldous and even today they still produce the traditional milk based 'Aldous' ice cream which tastes just like your grandma would remember it. The family recipe was handed down to Chris Coughlan when he bought the business in 1992 after he saw an advert in the Sunday Times. Since then the heritage brand has progressed in leaps and bounds.

Lakenham Creamery were the first in the UK to produce a super-premium ice cream. Their Norfolk County range is made with a fresh cream base, along with sugar, egg yolks and natural flavours, nothing more and nothing less, no extras and definitely no guar gum, carrageenan, or other stabilising ingredients which you'll find in many other ice cream brands.

It's an old fashioned yet effective way of making ice cream and exactly how you would do it at home but of course in commercial volumes. The exceptionally high cream content and traditional batch method of production creates a velvet smooth and decadent gourmet ice cream which has deservedly won over a whopping 120 awards.

"Our aim is to retain that authentic taste of ice cream and we do this by taking our time with the process, it makes a significant difference in the quality of the finished product which we take a huge amount of pride in. That's what we're all about and that's what keeps our customers coming back," says Chris.

They produce numerous enticing flavours including the safe options of French vanilla and Belgian chocolate but also lots of exotic flavours such as passion fruit, mango alphonse and coconut & cream. Their range has bagged them 28 Great Taste Awards and new flavours are continually being added to their roster including vanilla & pecan crunch, their seasonal flavour spiced orange & cranberry and mascarpone & fig which features in their recipe overleaf.

Lakenham Creamery were suppliers to Harrods for over 25 years. They now supply establishments from East Anglia into London including gastropubs, restaurants, farmshops, delis, hotels, local Waitrose branches and The Queen's Estate at Sandringham.

The small artisan business has come along way since 1921 and they don't plan on stopping any time soon. What's next on the agenda? Gooseberry & Elderflower.

ICE CREAM
SALES
ACROSS YARD

Lakenham Creamery
POACHED FIGS WITH MASCARPONE AND FIG ICE CREAM

This is a simple and delicious French style dessert which is an ideal fruit accompaniment to our mascarpone and fig ice cream. Great in late summer and autumn when figs are at their finest. Be sure to select figs which are purple and not overripe.

Preparation time: 10 minutes | Cooking time: 45 minutes | Serves 4

Ingredients

8 fresh figs

175ml Sauternes dessert wine

1 vanilla pod

A drizzle of honey or maple syrup

Method

Preheat the oven to 180°c.

Wash the figs and remove the stalk and any pips on the base. Then cut a cross slice from the top to the bottom to halfway down the body of the fig, pull out the 'leaves' to make a petal shape from the fig.

Pour the Sauternes into a small dish and remove the vanilla seeds from the pod before mixing these into the wine.

Place the figs in a small ovenproof dish bottom down. Pour the wine mixture over the centre of the figs making sure the liquid is deep enough to cover at least half the fig and place in the oven for 45 minutes. After 15 minutes of cooking, baste the figs with the wine every 10 minutes.

Allow to cool or chill completely before spooning the cold syrup over the figs and serving with our Norfolk County marscapone and fig ice cream. Add a drizzle of honey or maple syrup to finish.

Made to LAST

Nestled in the historic heart of Norwich, The Last Wine Bar and Restaurant is an independent family-run business built around good food, good wine and good old-fashioned hospitality.

When The Last Wine Bar and Restaurant opened its doors in 1990, owners James Sawrey-Cookson and Ecky Limon firmly placed the focus on a quality wine list, accompanied by some lovely plates of food. Over the last 25 years, The Last has gradually increased its culinary presence until the food has become as important, if not more important, than the wine.

The independent bar and restaurant is housed in a building that was once a nineteenth-century Victorian shoe factory. "Many of our customers don't realise that the name, The Last, comes from the name of the mould used to make shoes," Ecky explains.

In fact, if you look closely, James and Ecky have very much kept the history of the building alive, especially in the bar where many original features remain, such as the 'dispensing department' sign that hangs above the bar. You will even spot last light fittings and Singer sewing machine bases for the tables.

The small business has a strong ethos that comes from being proudly independent. "We are always striving to do the best we can," says Ecky, "even after 25 years, we are always pushing to do even better." Front of house manager, Emma Swatman, has been at the forefront of their renowned customer service for over 15 years. She knows many of their regular clientele by name and loves to welcome new customers, too.

The Last is now almost as well known for their food as for their carefully selected wine list. This is partly thanks to new head chef Iain McCarten, whose impressive career to date has influenced his love for foraging and sourcing local produce. He has been inspired by Norfolk's natural larder already, and is working hard to promote local and seasonal produce.

Having been around for a quarter of a century, The Last Wine Bar and Restaurant is a Norwich culinary institution. However, it has continually evolved and developed over time, and it will continue to be inspired by the people, city and county on its doorstep for a long time to come.

NORFOLK QUAIL WITH CELERIAC, OYSTER MUSHROOMS, APPLE AND A MADEIRA SAUCE

Iain McCarten became head chef at The Last Wine Bar at the start of 2017. Originally from Devon, he has been inspired by the bounty of Norfolk and uses a plethora of local produce in his dishes.

Preparation time: 30 minutes | Cooking time: 30 minutes | Serves 4

Ingredients

3 small celeriac

100ml single cream

100ml milk

4 whole Norfolk quail

2 sprigs of thyme

2 garlic cloves

4 Norfolk quail's eggs

2 potatoes

200ml vegetable oil

200g oyster mushrooms

200ml chicken stock

100ml Madeira

2 Granny Smith apples, peeled and chopped into matchsticks

1 truffle

Salt and pepper

Butter

Method

Preheat the oven to 180˚c.

Peel and halve two of the celeriac. Oil and season them, and place on a chargrill until nicely charred. Then place in the preheated oven until cooked through; this should take about 10 minutes.

Cut the third celeriac into small chunks and put into a pan with the cream and milk. Simmer until soft, then remove from the liquid and blitz in a food processor, adding back in some of the cream and milk mixture until smooth and silky. Season the purée to taste whilst in the blender.

Oil and season the quails and place into a hot frying pan with foaming butter, thyme sprigs and garlic cloves. Cook until golden brown, then finish in the oven for approximately 4 minutes, or until the bird is cooked and the juices run clear. Remove from oven and rest.

Place the quail's eggs into a pan of seasoned boiling water for 2 minutes 20 seconds. Remove from the pan and chill them in iced water, then peel off the shells.

Peel the potatoes, then using a vegetable spiraliser, spiralise them into potato spaghetti. Wrap this spaghetti around the quail's eggs so they are completely covered. Shallow fry these egg nests in a little vegetable oil until golden brown. Remove from the oil onto a kitchen towel, and season.

Clean the mushrooms with a pastry brush, removing any twigs or grit. Sauté them in some butter and seasoning.

Reduce the Madeira, and then the chicken stock. Reduce until thickened, and finish with a small cube of butter.

To assemble the dish, spoon the celeriac purée onto a warm plate and place the roasted celeriac on this. Remove the breasts and legs from the quail and arrange on the plate. Delicately place the crispy egg, oyster mushrooms and raw apple around the plate. Finish with the Madeira sauce and freshly shaved truffle.

Heart of THE VILLAGE

Old Hunstanton is home to The Lodge, a contemporary pub set within a historic building where the traditional and modern are beautifully combined.

Set within walking distance of the beautiful Norfolk coast, a sand dune beach and a golf club, The Lodge is nestled in the middle of the village of Old Hunstanton in a building that dates back more than 450 years. Its varied history, which includes intriguing stories of 18th-century smugglers, eventually led to the building becoming a hotel in 1912. Today it boasts 16 beautifully appointed rooms, a contemporary bar, separate restaurant and garden room.

The family-owned pub is a place for all seasons – a roaring fires provides a warming glow in the winter and a bright garden room and sunny outside area make the most of long summer days. A young, friendly team of staff help to create a vibrant and relaxed atmosphere whatever the season.

A good drinks list is at the heart of any good pub, and the team at The Lodge are really passionate about everything it serves. A range of craft beers, ales and lagers are available alongside hand-picked wines from independent merchants. When it comes to the wine, the team at The Lodge are more concerned about the character than the label, so their carefully

selected wine list is something they truly take pride in. Gins are also popular – and there are more than a few options to choose from with a particular focus on artisan gins.

The commitment to quality continues with the food too. Pub classics sit alongside creative seasonal specials, but what unites every dish is the choice of fresh ingredients from local suppliers. From starters to homemade desserts, everything is prepared fresh in the kitchen.

Recipes are made using the finest local produce but the flavours take inspiration from around the world. We're talking slow-roasted shoulder of Norfolk pulled pork for example, which is served with hot toasted sourdough, charred pineapple and fennel and celeriac coleslaw, or agnolotti of Norfolk chicken and roasted breast, which comes with baby vegetables and a roast chicken and tarragon emulsion. Stone-baked pizzas are also on offer, along with a collection of pub classics.

Simple, seasonal and served with a smile, it's a place where the whole family is sure to have a good time.

The Lodge

Oh, so MOORISH

Serving fresh, nutritious and tasty lunches from the heart of the Norwich Lanes, Moorish Falafel Bar has brought a little Middle Eastern flavour to the city.

When Samia King opened her vegetarian café Moorish Falafel Bar six years ago, she was one of the first businesses in Norwich to offer authentic, hand-made falafel. Although she had identified this gap in the local market, it was still a great achievement to see people queuing from the door at lunchtime from the very first day.

Moorish is based in the heart of the bustling Norwich Lanes, the thriving, trendy district that was named 'Great British High Street' in 2014.

"I love being part of this area," Samia says, "it is just the most perfect place for me to be based. There is a big community feel and so many great events happening all the time."

The ethos of Moorish Falafel Bar is very much based around sustainability. Samia tries to use locally sourced ingredients as much as she can and aims to choose sustainable and ethical options for all aspects of her business.

The menu is 100% vegetarian and it is predominantly vegan, too. The food is all cooked fresh every single day ready for the busy lunch rush. Falafels are served in a pitta or salad box and most people find it hard to resist adding an extra or two like feta, olives, baba-ganoush, tabbouleh and various other Mediterranean and Middle Eastern additions.

Although most people take their lunch away, there is seating inside for customers to enjoy their falafel on the premises if they are not in a rush. Perhaps washed down with fresh mint tea or homemade lemonade…

Samia also runs a separate catering company alongside Moorish Falafel Bar, and her love for Middle Eastern and Mediterranean cuisine shines through in her freshly prepared and flavour-packed catering menus too.

Moorish Falafel Bar

MOORISH TAGINE WITH BUTTERNUT SQUASH AND ONION GARNISH

You can make your own ras-el-hanout spice mix for this vegetable tagine, which will ensure your dish is packed with flavour.

Preparation time: 15 minutes | Cooking time: 40 minutes | Serves 4

Ingredients

For the onion garnish:

2 tbsp vegetable oil

2kg onions, sliced

Pinch of saffron

1 tsp ground turmeric

100g raisins

50g granulated sugar

50g toasted flaked almonds

For the tagine:

1kg butternut squash, diced into large chunks

4 garlic cloves, crushed

2 tbsp olive oil

4 tbsp vegetable oil

2 red onions, finely sliced

2 tbsp Ras-al-hanout spice mix (see right)

2 pints vegetable stock

1 tsp sea salt

1 tin chickpeas, drained

50g prunes

100g green olives

200g green beans, cut in half

1 red pepper, sliced

1 bunch of fresh coriander, finely chopped

To serve:

Couscous, flaked almonds and coriander

Method

For the onion garnish

Heat the oil in a frying pan on a low heat and add the sliced onions. After 5 minutes add all the other ingredients and keep on a low heat. Cook for 45 minutes-1 hour stirring regularly. Once caramelised, take off the heat and leave to cool.

For the tagine

While the onion garnish is cooking, you can make the tagine. Preheat the oven to 180°c. Put the butternut squash and garlic in a roasting tray and cover with the olive oil. Add a pinch of salt and roast in the preheated oven for 15 minutes. Meanwhile, heat the vegetable oil in a large pan and sauté the red onions. When the onion is soft add 2 tablespoons of the ras-el-hanout (see below). Cook for 10 minutes, stirring regularly.

Add the vegetable stock and salt. After 5 minutes add the chickpeas, prunes and olives. Simmer for 5 minutes and then add green beans, red pepper and roasted butternut squash. Cook for a further 5 minutes and remove from the heat.

Serve the tagine with the couscous and garnish with the onions, flaked almonds and coriander.

To make your own ras-el-hanout spice mix

Mix together 3 tsp ground cumin, 3 tsp ground coriander, 1 tsp ground ginger, 1 tsp ground cinnamon, ½ tsp ground black pepper, 2 tsp ground turmeric and 1 tsp ground paprika.

Food that cuts
THE MUSTARD

A family-run coffee shop that roasts its own coffee, Mustard Coffee Bar has become renowned for offering incredible coffee and so much more besides...

For Elaine and her family, choosing where to open their own coffee shop was a piece of cake. They loved the city of Norwich and were attracted to the historic Norwich Lanes. They were lucky enough to be able to open their café in the unique building that was home to the original Colman's Mustard shop – a lovely connection to the city's history, which also inspired their name!

Elaine runs the business with her husband Gerard. A true family affair, they are joined by son Sean, who also works alongside them. They were lucky enough to inherit their chef Shana from the previous business and together the whole team has worked to create a real family feel where their many regular customers are greeted on first-name terms.

The food is based around the bounty of Norfolk, using sustainable and seasonal ingredients from local suppliers. For this reason, the menu can change weekly, or even daily! There are always a few regulars on the menu though, such as the sausage rolls and Scotch eggs, which have gained quite a following – and even feature in the Lonely Planet guide!

However when it comes to their famed products, it is hard to beat the reputation of their coffee. They roast it themselves, so it is completely unique to Mustard Coffee Bar.

After a successful three years, Elaine and Gerard decided to open a second venue, this time in the University of East Anglia. A totally different space, this vibrant and modern coffee shop offers the same Mustard Coffee Bar quality but within the exciting and dynamic atmosphere of a university setting.

They have also expanded the business to offer inside and outside catering, from business lunches to wedding receptions, thanks to the growing reputation of their top-quality food and charming hospitality. When someone calls to enquire about catering (or anything else for that matter!), it will be Elaine or Gerard that they speak to, which means they always get the personal service this family-run coffee shop has become famous for.

Mustard Coffee Bar
NORFOLK STOUT CAKE

This cake is based on Guinness cake but uses Norfolk Stout. I use Panther's
Black Panther Stout, which gives a lovely chocolatey taste.

Preparation time: 15 minutes | Cooking time: 55 minutes | Serves 8-12

Ingredients

For the cake:

250ml Norfolk Stout

400g caster sugar

100g cocoa powder

250g unsalted butter

100ml buttermilk

2 free-range eggs

1 tsp vanilla essence

250g plain flour

2 tsp bicarbonate of soda

1 tsp salt

For the frosting:

125g unsalted butter

175g cream cheese

500g icing sugar

Cocoa powder, for dusting

Method

For the cake

Preheat the oven to 180°c. Grease and line a 20cm cake tin and place it on a baking tray.

Put the stout, sugar, cocoa powder and butter in a pan over a low heat and heat until everything is dissolved. Do not boil! Leave to cool.

In a bowl mix the buttermilk, eggs and vanilla essence. Add to the cooled cocoa mixture. Sieve in the flour, bicarbonate of soda and salt, and mix well until all the ingredients are combined. The mixture will appear very wet at this stage but don't panic! It is a batter-style cake but it can leak occasionally, which is why it's always best to place the cake tin on a baking tray.

Bake for 55 minutes or until a skewer comes out clean. Because it's a batter, it has a tendency to go quite 'crusty' on top. You can overcome this by covering with foil after 40 minutes. Leave to cool for at least 10 minutes before removing from the tin.

For the frosting

Prepare the frosting by mixing together all the frosting ingredients. Once the cake is completely cooled, cover the entire cake with the frosting and dust with cocoa powder.

By the beautiful SEA

The pursuit of happiness has become a modern quest. The harder we look, however, the more elusive it can seem. At Number 10 Sheringham, an intimate, welcoming restaurant on the Norfolk's coast, Sonya and Mustapha Fassih seem to have cracked it, though.

Since opening in 2005, number 10's adoption of the 'slow food' ethos beloved of our Italian cousins has seen them win hearts and minds in their namesake village from locals and visitors alike. The menu is based around the best local, seasonal produce – whether it's mussels from Morston or asparagus from local growers. As such, it changes every four to six weeks to represent the very pick of what's on offer. One might choose duck confit served with beetroot dressing followed by cod fillet served on spring onion risotto with a red pepper sauce or sea bass with roasted fennel, tomato, and ginger, perhaps followed by a rhubarb and ginger crème brûlée or chocolate tart.

But what sets No. 10 Sheringham apart is that very few places really invite you to linger and enjoy the whole experience of dining in quite the same way. Everything at No 10 Sheringham is made and cooked to order. The dining room is a place where you are encouraged to sit down, relax, and take your time. Once you've booked your table, it's yours for the evening. No rush, no fuss.

Supporting this experience are the husband-and-wife team of Sonya and Mustapha Fassih. Moving to Norfolk after many years living and working in London, including Mustapha's stints at Farringdon Street's Quality Chop House and the French House in Soho, the family settled in Sheringham. Mustapha's Moroccan heritage means that the best of British combines inventively with dishes like mackerel fillet served with couscous and harissa dressing and authentic tagine. Because the focus is on the diner, the menu can also be taken as a starting point for further adventures with flavours, with vegetarian, coeliac, and gluten-free variations available.

In an industry where turnover is a watchword – of establishments, of diners, of approaches to food – that No.10 Sheringham is thriving over a decade after it first opened is testament to its belief that good food is worth taking your time over...

Nº 10
Café ~ Restaurant

No. 10 Sheringham
SAUTÉED SEA BASS FILLET WITH CROMER CRAB AND STIFFKEY MUSSELS

This recipe uses some of our favourite North Norfolk ingredients in a combination of great flavours and textures that really celebrates our proximity to the sea.

Preparation time: 15 minutes | Cooking time: 40 minutes | Serves 6

Ingredients

For the sea bass:

6 sea bass fillets

Rapeseed oil (a dash)

Asparagus (a bunch)

For the crab cakes:

285g mashed potatoes

450g white crab meat

2tsp parsley, chopped

Plain flour (for dusting)

2 tbsp Bruniose of vegetables

For the mussels:

18 mussels, scrubbed, debearded

2 cloves garlic, peeled

1 shallot, peeled

4 sprigs of thyme

2 bay leaves

250ml dry white whine

250ml double cream

Method

Place the crabmeat and potatoes in a bowl. Mix together until evenly distributed.

Add the parsley and Bruniose of vegetables and mix well, cover and place in the fridge.

Put the mussels in a large pot with every ingredient bar the double cream. Cover and bring to the boil. Cook until the mussels are open.

Remove the mussels from the shells, put to one side.

Strain and reserve the cooking liquid into a small pan. Reduce to a glaze before adding the cream and continuing to reduce slowly.

Snap off and discard the bottom two-thirds of the asparagus steams, and peel the tips. Blanch in boiling water until tender, then remove and cool in ice-cold water

Place a splash of rapeseed oil in a frying pan to heat. Taking the crab mixture from the fridge, flour hands lightly and then shape palm-sized crab cakes by hand and sauté in hot oil for 2 minutes each side or until browned and hot through. Put to one side and keep warm.

Put the mussels back in the cream sauce and keep warm.

Removing the asparagus tips from the cold water, char-cook them on a hot griddle or alternatively fry gently in a little butter.

Over a medium heat, place the sea bass skin side down in the frying pan and press to keep the fillet flat and in full contact with the pan for 2-3 minutes approximately. Turn the fillets over to briefly cook the other side.

Placing the asparagus in the middle of a pre-warmed plate, place the crab cake on top, and then the sea bass on top of that. Carefully pour the mussels and sauce around the centred food.

Serve immediately. Bon Appétit!

Flying high at
NORFOLK QUAIL

For the Savory family of Highfield Farm, farming is much more than their business – it is a way of life and a passion, too.

John and Ellie Savory, along with their two children, are the fourth generation of the Savory family to farm Highfield Farm in the tranquil Wensum Valley. Highfield Farm has been known for its premium organic Soil Association-certified chicken eggs for 20 years, but today it is perhaps better known as the home of Norfolk Quail, which appears on top restaurant menus up and down the country.

The story of Norfolk Quail began in 2010 when John and Ellie were enjoying dinner in one of London's top restaurants. They were engaged in a conversation with the Maître d' about ingredients. As keen foodies themselves, as well as being farmers, they were intrigued about what ingredients chefs found it difficult to source within the UK. The Maître d' took them into the kitchen to talk to the chef, who revealed that one of the ingredients that the kitchen would love to be able to source in the country was quality British quail.

At the time, Ellie and John had been supplying their organic eggs to Waitrose, so they were already known for their commitment to producing food to the highest welfare standards – and, of course, to the highest quality.

They launched Norfolk Quail in 2011 with only 20 birds in a stable. The aim – to provide an English alternative to French quail meat. Their birds were free to fly and reared with the very best in care – they have room to forage and fly from the moment they hatch. This care and attention results in sweet, succulent and flavoursome meat that is perfect for roasting, barbecuing, pan-frying or baking.

The eggs, too, are a delight for chefs. Encased in attractive speckled shells, the bite-size morsels are ideal for creative cooks who use them in canapés, starters or salads. They are also regularly pickled or used as the basis of a mini Scotch egg. John and Ellie's children, Guy and Grace, will also agree that they are perfect for little appetites!

Although Norfolk Quail is now known all over the country, let's not forget that Highfield Farm still produces some of the country's finest chicken eggs. In fact, in 2016 they launched The Breckland Brown egg. Produced by free-range chickens that roam lush, sheltered grassland, this luxurious egg is rich in colour and flavour – the perfect ingredient for rich custard tarts or the perfect eggs Benedict.

Eric Snaith's Custard Tart

Norfolk Quail
NORFOLK QUAIL EGG

Chef Charlie Hodson created this recipe to showcase the Norfolk Quail egg. Norfolk Quail eggs are laid by free-to-fly hens, which are kept to the highest welfare standards.

Preparation time: 20 minutes | Cooking time: 10 minutes | Serves 6

Ingredients

6 Norfolk Quail eggs

2 good slices of Fruit Pig black pudding

450g sausage meat

20ml Wild Knight vodka (distilled with Norfolk barley and adds a smokey subtle undertone to the flavour)

Pinch of Maldon sea salt

Pinch of black ground pepper

1 coffee cup of plain flour

3 good-size chicken eggs, beaten

3 coffee cup of breadcrumbs

Crush Foods rapeseed oil, for deep-frying

Method

Preheat the oven to 160°c.

Place the quail eggs in boiling salted water for 2 minutes. Remove and place in cold water, peel and set aside.

Crumble the black pudding in your hands, but keeping the texture of finely diced onion. Mix with the sausage meat, Wild Knight vodka, salt and pepper, and split into six equal portions.

Place a quail egg into the centre of one portion of sausage meat mix, and gently mould the mix around the egg and shape into golf ball size. Repeat with the remaining eggs and sausage meat. Put the flour in one bowl, the beaten eggs in another bowl and the breadcrumbs in a third bowl. Roll the coated eggs in the flour, then the egg, then the crumbs.

Heat the oil to 180°c using a thermometer (which can be purchased from any good cook shop). Deep-fry the eggs until golden, then transfer to the oven for 5 minutes. And there we have the possibly the best Norfolk Quail egg!

What makes the difference in this recipe is not my skill (as it's really simple!), but it is the amazing produce available to myself and so many other chefs in Norfolk, which can all be found in our bountiful county.

CUSTARD TART

Eric Snaith of Titchwell Manor created this delicious pudding recipe with our Breckland Brown eggs.

Preparation time: 20 minutes | Cooking time: 40 minutes | Serves 6-8

Ingredients

For the pastry:

300g unsalted butter, cold and diced

450g plain flour

150g caster sugar

2 lemons, zest

6g salt

100g Breckland Brown whole egg

40g Breckland Brown egg yolk

For the filling:

1.25l whipping cream

410g Breckland Brown egg yolks

190g sugar

Nutmeg, to grate

Method

For the pastry

Preheat the oven to 120°c. Lightly rub the cold butter into the flour, sugar, zest and salt until it resembles fine breadcrumbs. Create a small dip in the middle of the bowl and add the Breckland Brown egg and yolk. Gently knead being careful not to overwork the pastry. Roll it out and line a 20cm tin.

For the filling

Warm the cream to around 80°c. Whisk the Breckland Brown egg yolks and sugar together, and temper with the cream. Pour into a jug.

To cook

Place the tart case into the preheated oven and fill with the filling, before finally grating a generous amount of nutmeg over the top of the tart. Bake for around 35-40 minutes, until there is a loose wobble in the centre.

Legendary SPIRIT

Striking drinks brand, Black Shuck, has taken the spirit of the county and bottled it in a unique range of local spirits and liqueurs.

Patrick and Sarah Saunders, together with their children Leanne, Nicola and William established The Norfolk Sloe Company in 2011 when they began making Black Shuck Sloe Gin and Black Shuck Sloe Gin Truffles. The business grew quickly with the introduction of other Black Shuck Liqueurs such as Blackcurrant Rum, Raspberry Vodka, Damson Port and Plum Brandy.

On December 1st 2015, after 2 years of recipe development and the taste-testing help of friends and family, they proudly launched Black Shuck Gin.

Black Shuck Gin, Norfolk's Legendary Spirit is strong and yet smooth, traditional and yet contemporary, complex and yet balanced. It has lightly floral notes from the Norfolk lavender followed by warm sweet fruity tones from the Sea Buckthorn and Bitter Orange Peel. It is cut to a final bottling ABV of 43% with Norfolk bore water.

Inspired by Norfolk, its silky character echoes the sweeping beaches, meandering inland waterways and easy-going lifestyle. Whilst its fresh lilac tones are reminiscent of the big skies, and the contrasting vibrant bursts of fiery orange reflect Norfolk's timeless natural beauty.

The logo, which was designed by Leanne to represent the iconic branding, is based around the Norfolk legend Black Shuck. A huge ghostly spirit dog with a black shaggy coat and flaming red eyes, Black Shuck is said to roam the East Anglian coast. No one knows for sure where Black Shuck came from and there are probably as many variations on the legend as there are varieties of gin!

Some people believe that the demon dog has its origins in Norse mythology, some even believe that it inspired Sir Arthur Conan Doyle's The Hound of the Baskervilles. Some tales recall Black Shuck as a protector to lone women, or a guide to lost travellers. However more sinister stories depict Black Shuck as a bad omen who will bring ill fate to anyone who sees him…

You will therefore be pleased to learn that in the event that you should meet Black Shuck , The Norfolk Sloe Company can provide an antidote. According to the family-run company, a single glass of Black Shuck gin will fill you with enough good spirit to overcome any bad spirits you may encounter!

The Norfolk Sloe Company
BLACK SHUCK GIN AND TONIC

According to Winston Churchill, 'The Gin and Tonic has saved more Englishmen's lives and minds than all the doctors in the British Empire.' He was referring to the discovery that quinine, a fundamental ingredient of tonic, is an effective treatment against malaria. British officers in India added gin to their tonic to make it more palatable. Hence the Gin and Tonic was born.

Preparation time: 1 minute | Serves 1

Ingredients

25ml Black Shuck Gin

50-100ml tonic water

Orange zest, to garnish

Ice

Method

Add a handful of cubed ice to a large balloon glass. Pour over a measure of Black Shuck Gin. Add your favourite tonic water. We recommend Fever Tree Indian Tonic. Garnish with a twirl of orange zest and serve.

BLACK SHUCK GIN GENIE COCKTAIL

It is said that the first cocktails were invented by alchemists trying to find a recipe for eternal life! The term 'cocktail' possibly comes from the early nineteenth century, when an American bartender garnished a drink with the tail feather of a rooster. The Black Shuck Gin Genie combines some of Patrick and Sarah's favourite ingredients and is their own tribute to David Bowie's Jean Genie.

Preparation time: 1 minute | Serves 1

Ingredients

25ml Black Shuck Gin

10ml pomegranate and elderflower cordial

1 tsp pomegranate seeds

70ml prosecco

Method

Fill a large balloon glass with cubed ice. Pour over a measure of Black Shuck Gin. Add a generous splash of pomegranate and elderflower cordial. Sprinkle over a teaspoonful of pomegranate seeds and top with prosecco. Serve.

Flower POWER

Dr Sally Francis wanted to be a farmer since she was a little girl; she now grows the world's most precious spice on the Norfolk Coast.

It all began with Sally's mother Jill buying 20 saffron corms for her as a birthday present in 1997. Sally looked after the crops for years which multiplied to the point where she was giving saffron away to friends and family, soon they had so much that they decided to sell some at farmers' markets. They were astounded by the enthusiastic response and with the help of RDPE funding, Norfolk Saffron was born.

Norfolk Saffron's HQ is based on the North Norfolk coast where barn owls, hares, marsh harriers and other charming rare species regularly visit. Botanist Sally is big on protecting the environment, which is why they use recyclable packaging and avoid herbicides, fungicides or pesticides on their crops. "We look after our soil properly, building up and maintaining fertility whilst preventing compaction and erosion. The saffron is grown in a crop rotation to make it sustainable - one harvest a year for 4-6 weeks" sally said.

Her saffron is incredibly potent and of the highest quality so a little goes a really long way. Every year they send the saffron to an independent laboratory in France for a quality test which isn't often done by other saffron producers. There are three grades of strength and Sally has produced the very best

every single time. During harvesting, Norfolk Saffron only picks the rich, red part of the stigma because that is where all the characteristic saffron colour, flavour and aroma is. No machinery exists that can harvest saffron; everything is done by hand which is why genuine saffron always comes at a price.

Most people use saffron in savoury dishes such as paella or risotto but Sally likes to experiment with sweet recipes such as saffron ice-cream or indulgent saffron buns which you can create yourself using the traditional recipe overleaf. Saffron flour can be purchased from their online shop and from Sally's stockists, along with orange & saffron liqueur and smoked saffron threads which have all won Great Taste awards.

Have a go at using these amazing ingredients yourself at home, or at the cookery demonstrations Sally is developing. The history of saffron is fascinating and you can learn all about the unique spice at their pop-up Saffron Museum – the only museum dedicated to saffron in the UK!

Who knew that the little birthday present from years ago would lead to her becoming an award-winning leading commercial saffron producer?

Norfolk Saffron
INDULGENT SAFFRON BUNS

In the not-so-distant past, before chocolate took over, saffron was the flavour of Easter and saffron buns were always baked. This recipe is based on one from the Georgian period. Enjoy these golden buns not only at Easter, but on lazy Sunday morning breakfasts too, or toasted in front of a roaring fire for tea.

Preparation time: 30 minutes plus proving time | Cooking time: 10-20 minutes | Makes 12

Ingredients

500g strong white Norfolk Saffron Flour

50g sugar

1½ tsp salt

2 tsp easy-blend yeast

2 free-range eggs, room temperature

200ml whole milk, lukewarm

75g butter, melted

Method

Firstly, get a large bowl and blend together the Norfolk Saffron Flour, sugar, salt and yeast.

In a separate bowl, beat the eggs before mixing in the milk and melted butter. Then add this to the dry mixture to create a dough. Knead for 10 minutes until it becomes smooth and elastic.

Set the dough aside in a warm place, allowing it to rise until it has doubled in size. Being an enriched dough, it can take longer to prove than ordinary bread dough.

Once ready, knock it back, weigh the dough and divide into 12 equal pieces (or more if you want smaller rolls).

Form the dough pieces into rolls and then place on an oiled baking sheet, approximately a centimetre apart. Sprinkle them with flour and put in a warm place once again, loosely covered with a cloth. Meanwhile, preheat the oven to 220°c.

Allow to rise until the rolls are touching.

Bake in the oven for 10-20 minutes until golden.

These buns freeze well, so can be baked in advance if required.

Ollands Farm Foods
SMOKED SALMON AND BEETROOT BLINIS

Mary Ann and Kim started their preserves business at the beginning of 2013 starting off small with local farmers' markets. Ollands Farm Foods went from strength to strength, growing the business together to what it is now – an award-winning jam, marmalade, pickle and chutney producer who promote the excellence of Norfolk produce by sourcing their ingredients locally where they can. Everything is made by hand using traditional artisan methods and they carry out every step of the process themselves. Every year they introduce new items to their extensive range, some of which become bestsellers such as their Seville Orange Marmalade, Lime & Chilli Marmalade and Lemon & Herb Marmalade which all won a Gold Award at the World Marmalade Awards 2017.

This quick and easy recipe makes delicious canapés ideal for entertaining or simply a weekend treat. The Beetroot & Orange Chutney provides the perfect complement to the richness of the salmon and crème fraîche. This recipe uses half-fat crème fraîche but it can be made with the full fat variety if preferred. Serve with a glass of sparkling prosecco or your favourite cocktail. They can be prepared in advance and kept in the fridge for up to an hour. Smoked trout can also be used as an alternative to salmon, if you are looking for a more earthy flavour.

Preparation time: 10 minutes | Cooking time: 5 minutes | Serves 4

Ingredients

1 pack small ready-made blinis

100g smoked salmon

200g half-fat crème fraîche

1 jar Ollands Farm Foods Beetroot & Orange Chutney

Method

Take blinis out of packaging and warm up in an oven at 120°c for approximately five minutes. Whilst they heat up, cut the smoked salmon into bite-sized pieces (around 2cm x 4cm).

Once the blinis are out of the oven, place a generous teaspoon of crème fraîche on to each. Then place a piece of chopped salmon on top of the crème fraîche.

Finish off with a dollop of Ollands Farm Foods Beetroot & Orange Chutney and voila!

ChilliLilli

Strawberry Jam

Raspberry Jam

Farm to FORK

The award-winning pub and restaurant with rooms, Recruiting Sergeant, is well known in the area around Horstead for its fabulous food and friendliness.

Recruiting Sergeant is a village pub with a lot of heart. Run by Nicola and Matthew Colchester, its reputation for good beers, great food and friendly service has travelled much further afield than Horstead – in fact it is renowned throughout the county.

Credited by CAMRA, Recruiting Sergeant is known for the well-kept ales behind the bar and the pub features in The Good Beer Guide 2017 thanks to the array of beers on offer.

As far as the food is concerned, Recruiting Sergeant is all about serving up the best that Norfolk has to offer – and that is something pretty special. The team has a close relationship with Swannington Farm to Fork, which is based only nine miles away. This multi award-winning business has been rearing animals to the highest welfare standards since 1973.

The meat from Swannington isn't the only local produce to feature on the menus. Fresh fish and seasonal vegetables are sourced from the county, too, meaning that the restaurant changes its specials with the seasons, so there is always something new to try.

The commitment to good food continues over the road where their deli showcases even more of Norfolk's impressive

ingredients. The deli, which is called From Farm to Fork and Fish, is run by Nicola and Matthew along with Rob Mutimer of Swannington Farm to Fork. It comprises a butchery, fishmonger and deli counter.

The array of meat features seasonal lamb, prime beef, outdoor-reared pork, free-range poultry, award-winning sausages, their own dry-cured bacon and ham, and their famous sausage rolls and pâtés, as well as some gluten-free sausages and burgers, too. Fresh fish and shellfish is sourced daily by Matthew, who is famous for his approach to cooking with fresh, seasonal produce. He and the team are on hand to give advice to customers, too, as they endeavour to make fresh seafood accessible to everyone.

The deli is packed with all sorts of Norfolk goodies, from cheese, eggs, charcuterie, chutneys and vegetables to homemade quiches, pies, bread, cakes and ready-meals.

Between the deli and the pub, they have created a little foodie paradise in the village and secured Horstead's place firmly on the Norfolk foodie map.

Recruiting Sergeant
SPICY BBQ BEEF RIBS

One of our favourite dishes. Succulent beef short ribs are slow-cooked to tender perfection and coated in a sticky BBQ sauce.

Preparation time: 20 minutes | Cooking time: 4-5 hours | Serves 2

Ingredients

4 beef short ribs, approximately 200g each

2 tbsp English mustard powder

2 tbsp smoked paprika

4 tbsp dark muscovado sugar

1 fresh red chilli, sliced

2 star anise

1 pint cola

1 pint Woodfordes ale

For the BBQ Sauce:

300ml ketchup

250mls soy sauce

50g English mustard

100g honey

150g dark muscovado sugar

Thumb-size piece of ginger, grated

4 cloves garlic

25ml sweet chilli sauce

For the garnish:

Finely sliced red peppers

Finely sliced spring onions

Finely sliced chillies

Method

Preheat the oven to 125°c. Place the beef short ribs into a tray and coat with the dry ingredients. Scatter the chilli and star anise around the edge. Pour the cola and beer into the tray, cover with foil and bake for 3-4 hours, until tender.

Blitz together the BBQ sauce ingredients.

Strain the liquid from the ribs into a pan and reduce by half. Add the blended BBQ sauce ingredients and cook down until it is the consistency of double cream.

Increase the oven temperature to 180°c. To finish the ribs, place them on a baking tray and pour the sauce over. Roast in the oven for 20 minutes to glaze.

Place the ribs nicely on a plate and garnish the top with finely sliced red peppers, spring onions and chillies.

Relaxed ELEGANCE

The well-established restaurant Roger Hickman's has been flying the flag for modern British fine dining in Norfolk for over seven years.

Roger Hickman's history in Norwich goes back much further than the restaurant itself. He had been working as head chef in the same kitchen he now calls his own, long before his name appeared above the door.

He earned his reputation for fine cuisine when the restaurant was the legendary Adlard's, having also previously worked in an impressive array of fine-dining and Michelin-starred kitchens. When he transformed the restaurant into Roger Hickman's seven years ago, he cemented his place as one of Norfolk's best-loved chefs.

The stylish interior has the refined elegance that you would expect from a restaurant with three AA rosettes. The crisp white table linens provide the perfect backdrop to Roger Hickman's contemporary British dishes, but he has put a lot of emphasis into creating a relaxed atmosphere too.

It is important to Roger that the service is as good as the food, and the restaurant has become well-known for its impeccable front of house service. About fifty percent of the restaurant's visitors are returning customers and regular diners, which goes to show that their approach is working.

As far as the food is concerned, Roger concentrates on sourcing the best produce he can from a medley of Norfolk producers. From Norfolk quail to Brancaster mussels, and from seasonal asparagus to freshly caught crab, the ingredients used paint a picture of the county's landscape. There is a focus on classic cooking in Roger's kitchen, but there are also creative twists aplenty.

Roger doesn't like to 'play around' too much with ingredients, which is understandable when you see the top-quality produce he is using. "If you are using the best ingredients, they speak for themselves," he says, as he explains why he likes to keep his dishes recognisable and accessible to diners.

As well as being passionate about cooking, Roger is also really interested in wine, and this is reflected in the award-winning wine list. The quirky list contains over 150 wines – and Roger can say he has tasted every single one. He has travelled to vineyards around Europe sampling the finest vintages before carefully selecting the bottles to serve in his restaurant, so diners can rest assured that they will be able to choose the perfect wine to accompany their meal.

Roger Hickman's
SMOKED AND CURED MACKEREL WITH GOOSEBERRY PURÉE

This recipe shows how to serve mackerel two ways. The textures work well together and the strong flavours really complement the sharpness of the gooseberries. Try to use fresh, locally sourced, sustainable fish wherever possible. Gooseberries can be exchanged for most sharp-tasting fruit, so depending on the season you can use apple or rhubarb. The mackerel will need 24 hours to cure in the fridge, so you will need to prepare this the night before.

Preparation time: 45 minutes, plus 24 hours curing | Serves 4

Ingredients

For the cured mackerel:

100g sugar

75g coarse salt

Bunch of dill, finely chopped

10g black pepper, crushed

4 mackerel fillets

For the mackerel mousse:

300ml cream

4 smoked mackerel fillets, skinned

1½ lemons, juice

1 gelatine leaf, soaked

Handful of chopped chives

Pinch of salt

For the gooseberry purée:

500g gooseberries

75g sugar

To garnish:

Fresh gooseberries

Radish

Deep-fried rice noodles

Method

For the cured mackerel

Mix the sugar, salt, dill and pepper together. Cover the mackerel fillets with the cure mixture and leave in the fridge for 24 hours. Wash off the cure and dry.

For the mackerel mousse

Whisk the cream to soft peaks. Mix the fish and lemon juice in a blender. Pass this through a sieve, then add the salt and soaked gelatine. Fold into the cream and add the chives.

For the gooseberry purée

Heat the gooseberries and the sugar until soft. Blitz this in a blender, then pass it through a sieve and chill.

To serve

Serve the cured mackerel with the mackerel mousse and gooseberry purée, garnished with fresh gooseberries, radish and deep fried rice noodles (seaweed powder can be used to season the rice noodles).

Spectacular VIEWS

"Once I stepped onto those terraces and saw the amazing views of the cathedral and castle, it did not take long to think of opening up the space as a restaurant. The views are so spectacular they had to be shared," says the proprietor Antonia.

Rooftop Gardens is a unique venue like no other, a sophisticated restaurant with two outdoor rooftop terraces, the first rooftop venue in the city in fact which successfully brings a flavour of London to Norwich. Aesthetically, the building is very typical of the time period in which it was constructed, the geometric concrete exterior is exemplary of early 1970s brutalist architecture, a rarity in Norwich, as it is one of few retained buildings of this type.

The restaurant, described as 'casual fine dining' has an innovative menu that is ever-changing. Head chef, Andrew Clegg found his passion for cooking at an early age. Inspired by his Nanny Brenda when he was a child, he was cooking meals for his family by the age of 13, so it's safe to say that you'll be well catered for! Andrew's aim is to create flavoursome and interesting courses with seasonal produce. Some of the popular dishes are crispy salt and pepper squid, whole roasted fish, pan roasted chicken supreme, anything off their Norfolk beef menu and the chef's favourite - slow braised shoulder of lamb which you can recreate yourself using the recipe overleaf. As you may have gathered, the food is by no means ordinary. This is partly because they are a firm advocate in sourcing locally, they strive to buy the best of locally grown and farmed produce to ensure freshness and reduce carbon footprint.

The stylish, urban and edgy eatery combined with the 360° panoramic views of Norwich's skyline creates an unrivalled ambience. In winter the covered terrace is cosy with heaters and blankets and in summer you can enjoy delectable cocktails under the heat of the sun. Whether you're a fine wine drinker or someone who prefers a pint of draught lager, this is the place you want to be. Especially as they plan to launch a high-end afternoon tea menu in 2017 to match some of London's finest. There will be an assortment of tastes and textures to indulge in, the most delectable sweet and savoury delights will of course be teamed with hot drinks, presented in fine bone china for that elegant touch.

Rooftop Gardens is the kind of place you can spend all evening in, start with post-work cocktails at the bar before moving onto a scrumptious dinner, and then perhaps a coffee or a digestif on the terrace sitting under the stars watching the lights of the city.

ROOFTOP GARDENS

Rooftop Gardens

SLOW BRAISED LAMB SHOULDER, SPRING ONION & POMEGRANATE QUINOA, CUMIN HUMMUS AND PISTACHIO ANCHOÏADE

We source our lamb from Swannington farm to fork who have 400 sheep on their farm, Rob at Swannington has a real passion for his animals. You can go there and see that they are happy, and when your meat is well cared for that is ultimately evident in both the flavour and quality of the meat.

Lamb is often perceived as fatty and unhealthy so with this recipe we have slow braised it, which removes some of the fat but retains enough to achieve maximum flavour. A slow braise also gives plenty of time to prepare everything else to accompany our beautiful piece of meat – we have gone for healthy ingredients such as quinoa, kale, pomegranate and pistachio nuts.

Preparation time: 30 minutes | Cooking time: 2.5-3 hours | Serves 4

Ingredients

Norfolk lamb shoulder

1 carrot, peeled

1 white onion, peeled

1 garlic clove

1 celery stick, peeled

1½ bottles red wine

350g quinoa

1.2 litres vegetable stock

60g pistachio nuts

40g anchovy fillets

200ml Norfolk rapeseed oil

2 lemons, juiced

250g kale

100g hummus

1 tsp toasted cumin seeds

Salt and pepper

1 bunch of spring onions, chopped

Handful of pomegranate seeds

Method

Preheat the oven to 140°c.

Place the lamb shoulder in a deep ovenproof dish along with the carrot, onion, garlic, celery and red wine, then cover with parchment paper and tin foil. Place the tray into the oven for 2.5 to 3 hours or until you can pull the meat apart easily with a fork.

Wash the quinoa under cold water to help remove any bitter taste, drain and add to another ovenproof dish along with the vegetable stock. Cover with parchment paper and bake for 12–20 minutes or until all the stock has evaporated and the quinoa is tender with just a little bite.

Place the pistachio nuts, anchovy fillets, rapeseed oil and lemon juice into a food processer and blitz until smooth.

Cook the kale in salted boiling water until tender, then drain and season.

To plate

Smear the hummus across the side of the bowl and top with some toasted cumin seeds. Fluff up the quinoa with a fork, season and fold through the spring onions and pomegranate seeds, put a generous couple of spoons of this alongside the hummus then top with the seasoned kale.

Pull the lamb shoulder apart with two forks and place on top of the kale then dress with the anchoïade, garnish with any remaining spring onions and pomegranate seeds.

Down on the FARM

Samuel's Farm Shop may be newly established, but it is built on traditional values...

Until recently Britain's Lord Chancellor used to sit on the Woolsack, a large sack of wool covered in red cloth, when in office. It was a tradition instituted in the Middle Ages, to remind people that Britain's wealth and eminence grew on the backs of its sheep. We've moved on since then. But Samuel's Farm Shop recognises that Norfolk's land still has a rich bounty to offer.

This isn't an establishment that pays lip-service to the idea of being family-run affair that uses locally-sourced produce. They're ideals that run through everything the business does. Take the shop itself. Launched in 2015, owner Ben Human built it with his own hands on the site of an old greenhouse on his family's farm so that he could showcase the very best of what it had to offer. What's on offer is food done the old-fashioned way: fresh, local, seasonal. It isn't just a point of pride that the shop's chicken, turkey, and lamb are reared on the surrounding farm, but also that the delicious pies and pastries are made onsite to traditional home-cooked recipes.

"We wanted to get back to traditional values," explains Ben. "Honest food that comes straight from the land and recipes that are as close to homemade as you can get. We wanted to put all of that together in a shop where people find a warm welcome, where they're treated as valued friends rather than just customers."

Because what's on the shelves of the shop comes from the fields of the farm, the seasonal, local approach of Samuel's Farm Shop means that customers get the very best produce at its freshest. The shop also supplies the best of an outstanding crop of local suppliers, such as Scotts Field's rare breed pork, biscuits from Cartwright and Butler, and local cheeses to go on them. All meat is sourced locally and to the highest standard, for example, with a real pride taken in ensuring that customers are provided with a wide range of essential items for everyday as well as special occasions: fresh bread, cakes, biscuits, milk, cheese, freshly made ready-meals, sweets, chutneys, and jams jostle for space with the best of seasonal fruit and vegetables.

It isn't just that the produce and food is of the highest quality. There's a real family friendly atmosphere at Samuel's Farm Shop. Family-run, it's also family-orientated, something as important to the shop as the food and produce on offer.

Samuel's Farm Shop

SAMUEL'S Barnsley Chop
£11.00 Per Kg

Samuel's Farm Shop

SAMUEL'S OWN STEAK, STILTON AND GUINNESS PIE

This is an example of one of our homemade recipes in action, and a real favourite with our customers!

Preparation time: 20 minutes | Cooking time: 1 hour 40 minutes | Serves 6

Ingredients

For the filling:

500g steak, cubed

100g onions, diced

1 tsp rosemary

1 tsp sage

1 tsp sugar

150ml of beef stock

200ml of Guinness

100g of Stilton

Plain for flour, for dusting

Oil, for frying

For the pastry:

200g of flour (soft)

A pinch of salt

50g of lard

50g of butter

2-3 tbsp Water

Method

To prepare the meat

Coating the meat lightly in a little plain flour, brown it in a heavy-based pan using a little oil.

Add the onions, rosemary, sage, sugar, beef stock, and Guinness and simmer on a low heat.

After 45 minutes add the Stilton and cook for a further 30 minutes until the meat is tender.

To prepare the pastry

Sieve the flour and salt into a suitable bowl.

Rub the fat in with the flour using your fingers until it creates a sandy texture.

Once done, make a well in the centre.

Add water into the well, mixing and adding a little more, and mixing further until a smooth paste has been created.

Preheat oven to 180°c.

Set aside one-third of the pastry for the lid. Roll out the larger portion of pastry on a flour-dusted surface.

Line a suitable pie dish with the pastry mix, pushing firmly into the surface of the tin until it meets the contours of the dish.

Fill the dish with the filling, and then top with the remaining pastry.

Brush the pastry with milk and bake in a moderate oven for 20-25 minutes, or until the pastry is golden brown and the filling is piping hot.

Showcasing NORFOLK

The produce shop at Wroxham Barns is not only the home of The Norfolk Sausage Company, but a treasure trove of gastronomic goodies from the county... welcome to Scrummy Pig.

Mike and Sam Fish have been running the award-winning produce shop at Wroxham Barns since it opened in October 2015. However, the start of their foodie journey actually began about 20 years ago when they were inspired to rear a couple of Gloucester Old Spot pigs and produce their own sausages...

The Norfolk Sausage Company was born in 2006 and their sausages have become firm favourites in the local community. Fast-forward to 2015 and Mike and Sam's business was forced out of its home due to a fire in the building, an unfortunate turn of events which had a happy outcome by leading them to their new home at Wroxham Barns.

When they opened Scrummy Pig – aptly named thanks to their delicious pork products! – they spent the first year talking to customers to find out what people wanted from the shop and gradually building up stock levels. They found that people wanted to buy local Norfolk produce – whether that be store-cupboard basics or gourmet gifts.

It is fair to say that Mike and Sam have never looked back. Scrummy Pig is a Norfolk food-lover's paradise – jam-packed with bacon, sausages, charcuterie, cheeses, artisan breads, marinades, chutneys, jams and all manner of other delights. From the amazing selection, they make bespoke Norfolk produce hampers for customers. Myriad local spirits, wines and more than 150 Norfolk beers makes it a unique shopping destination for drink-lovers too – it boasts Norfolk's largest collection of local bottled beers!

They are so passionate about the food and drink they stock, that they offer numerous products on a daily basis at their in-shop tasting bar. A rotating selection of some of Norfolk's finest produce, one day people might be sampling local beers alongside Norfolk mustards and regional flavoured rapeseed oils, whilst the next day could see spirits, jams and chutneys being sampled... whatever products are taking centre stage, you can be sure they will be made within the county.

They were over the moon to win Best New Food or Drink Venture at the Norfolk Hero Food and Drink Awards 2016 within a year of opening, and were also the first shop to be recognised as part of the Proudly Norfolk Food & Drink scheme. With 95% of their products sourced from within the county, this family-run shop has a big voice when it comes to championing Norfolk's amazing produce.

Scrummy Pig has just taken on its first apprentice in the form of Mike and Sam's daughter Jewelene – proof that a passion for good local food runs in the family!

Scrummy Pig

Scrummy Pig

PAN-ROASTED CHICKEN BREAST, PEARL BARLEY AND KALE RISOTTO AND SPICED CARROT CHUTNEY

Deciding whose product to feature in our recipe wasn't going to be easy given the sheer number of Norfolk products we stock. As it turned out there was one obvious choice – Candi's Chutney. What's more, Candi, being a professionally trained chef, kindly offered to design our recipe as well as cook it for us. Scale this recipe up depending on how many people you are serving.

Preparation time: 10 minutes | Cooking time: 30 minutes | Serves 1

Ingredients

2 tbsp Crush Rapeseed Oil

1 chicken breast (preferably on the bone as this adds flavour to the meat during cooking)

3 spring onions, finely chopped

1 clove garlic, finely chopped

115g pearl barley, lightly rinsed under cold water

1½ pints chicken stock

115g Norfolk-grown kale, tear off the thicker stalks

40ml Norton's Dairy double cream

1 tbsp Candi's Chutney spiced carrot chutney

Salt and black pepper

Method

Preheat the oven to 180°c. Add 1 tablespoon of Crush Rapeseed Oil to an oven-proof pan. Lightly season the chicken breast with salt and black pepper and place skin-side down into the pre-warmed pan on a medium heat. Once browned, carefully turn over and lightly brown the reverse side. Once both sides are lightly browned place into the oven and allow to finish cooking, approximately 25-30 minutes.

Whilst the chicken is finishing in the oven, it is time to make the risotto. Into a deep pan place the spring onions, garlic and remaining rapeseed oil, and cook these without colouring for approximately 3-4 minutes or until softened.

Add all of the pearl barley and stir well to ensure each grain is covered in the flavoured oil. Then pour in a pint of the chicken stock all at once. The joy of this risotto is that it is not as demanding as a traditional risotto, but tastes just as good, with an amazing texture. Stir well and turn the heat down to a medium heat and cook for approximately 15 minutes, stirring often. You are looking for a consistency of custard, not too thick but not too thin!

After 15 minutes of cooking add all the kale and again stir through and continue to cook for another 10-15 minutes. At this point you may need to add more stock, remember we want the consistency of a thick custard.

After the final cooking time add the Norton's double cream, stir through and season to taste. Remove from the heat and warm your serving bowl.

Remove the chicken from the oven and ensure it is cooked thoroughly, you can do this by checking the juices run clear when pierced with a sharp knife. Allow to rest.

Take the warmed serving bowl and into this place the pearl barley and kale risotto, top this with the pan-roasted chicken breast and gently top with Candi's Chutney spiced carrot chutney. Pour a glass of chilled Pinot Grigio, sit back and enjoy!

Award-winning
PRESERVES

Making jams and marmalade in the age-old way has led to award success for Ali from Season's Bounty, who has accumulated a plethora of awards for her hand-made Norfolk preserves.

Like many successful businesses, Season's Bounty came about by accident rather than design. Its founder, Ali Barwick, had been a keen preserve-maker for many years, having grown up in a family who simply loved to cook and bake.

The inspiration to turn her hobby into a business came from a trip to a farmers' market in 2013. Admiring a stall full of homemade preserves, she wondered if she could do the same with her own and supplement the income from her then business as a gardener. After all, she had been giving most of them away to friends and family for years.

Quite simply, Season's Bounty took off from day one. People loved her traditionally made preserves, and the time she spent on her new business gradually increased until she was doing it full-time and had to give up her gardening altogether.

A one-woman business, Ali started off in her home kitchen and is entirely self-taught. As demand increased, she moved into a purpose built kitchen to allow her to increase her production rate, but Ali still continues to hand-cut all the fruit for her marmalades, and hand prepares all the fruit for her jams. Everything is then cooked in traditional maslin pans.

The array of awards that Season's Bounty has achieved is impressive to say the least. She won her first Great Taste Award for her Strawberry and Elderflower Jam in 2014, followed by another in 2015 for her Strawberry Jam with Norfolk Lavender.

Her marmalades have also achieved a string of accolades at the World Original Marmalade Awards, which are held in Cumbria every March. In 2017, she was awarded three gold, six silver and two bronze medals, which she can add to her tally of four golds, three silvers and five bronzes.

From foraging in the hedgerows and picking her own fruit, Ali takes great pride in using the best local ingredients. Whether the produce comes from her allotment or from local farms, and orchards, what goes into Ali's preserves depends almost entirely on the season's bounty.

Season's Bounty
SPICED MARMALADE CAKE

Although I make preserves for a living (which I love doing), a very close second is baking. For The Norfolk Cook Book, I have created a cake recipe that uses one of my award-winning marmalades. The method is very similar to that of a gingerbread and is very easy.

Preparation time: 20 minutes | Cooking time: 1 hour | Serves 16

Ingredients

175g butter

110g Demerara sugar

110g light soft brown sugar

175g golden syrup

1 jar Season's Bounty Old Fashioned Seville Marmalade

450g plain wholemeal flour

15ml baking powder

5ml bicarbonate of soda

5ml ground cinnamon

5ml ground ginger

5ml ground nutmeg

1 large egg

250ml milk

Method

Line a 23cm square baking tin with baking paper. Preheat the oven to 180°c (170°c fan/350°F/Gas 4). Warm the butter, sugars, syrup and marmalade together in a saucepan until the butter has melted.

In a bowl, sift together the remaining dry ingredients. Beat the egg together with the milk.

Add the melted ingredients into the dry ingredients and mix well, but gently. Then add the milk and egg mixture and stir in well. The mixture will be a soft pouring consistency. Pour the mixture into the prepared tin and bake in the oven for about 1 hour, or until well risen and just firm to the touch.

Leave in the tin for about 20 minutes before turning out onto a cooling rack. Remove the baking paper once cold. Store in an airtight container.

Deliciously DIFFERENT

When it comes to unusual places to enjoy fabulous food, it doesn't come much more enticing than a cosy, rustic yurt... welcome to Shuck's.

Philip and Beth Milner fell in love with the unique yurt at Drove Orchards in Thornham at first sight. Philip had been working as a head chef along the Norfolk coast for over 20 years and had accrued various awards, such as Seafood Chef of the Year and Pub Chef of the Year, throughout his career.

When he and Beth decided to open their own restaurant, they had a strong idea in their minds about what sort of place they wanted to create. They wanted it to be an eatery where everyone was welcome, including families and their four-legged friends, and the yurt struck them as the ideal space.

They have named their restaurant after the mythical black hound that was said to wander the Norfolk coast – a legend with a bit of a bite, it seemed the perfect fit! Within two months they were featured in the Waitrose Good Food Guide for 2017 as a reader recommended restaurant, thanks to their relaxed dining experience and excellent food.

The menu reflects the landscape around them as they make the most of the wonderful produce from Drove's fruit orchards and kitchen gardens, alongside seafood from the coast and other produce from local suppliers. They aim for unpretentious dishes and honest, rustic food, but Philip's creativity in the kitchen means there are plenty of unexpected twists. He is known for his love of spice, and the Shuck's weekly curry night has become a popular event. So much so, he is thinking about launching his own curry paste.

The end of 2016 saw Shuck's win the PRS Music Makeover competition, which included £5,000 worth of music equipment, a bespoke music consultation from producer Steve Levine and an exclusive launch event. This exciting development has enabled them to host local bands at Shuck's – and what goes better with great food than great music? There are plans for a family music festival in the summer, too.

There are also plans in the pipeline for a new chicken shack and rustic pizza takeaway, cementing Shuck's place as a relaxed foodie haven for families in Norfolk. While the little ones entertain themselves in the kid's corner, grown-ups can relax in front of the log burner in winter or outside in the summer and enjoy delicious food and drink in this beautiful corner of Norfolk.

SHUCK'S

Shuck's
SALT MARSH LAMB

This recipe showcases salt marsh lamb with seared loin, crispy belly and faggot, accompanied by Jerusalem artichokes and crispy goat's cheese cannelloni.

Preparation time: 1 hour, plus 1 hour chilling | Cooking time: 4-5 hours | Serves 4

Ingredients

For the artichoke:

10 Jerusalem artichokes (8 for purée, 2 for crisps)

½ pint milk

70g butter

1 vegetable stock cube

Splash of truffle oil (optional)

Salt and pepper

Oil, for deep-frying

For the cannelloni:

1 small log of goat's cheese, peeled

100g sun-blushed tomatoes

Bunch of basil

70ml double cream

1 pack fresh lasagne sheets

1 egg, beaten

Oil, for deep-frying

For the lamb:

1 belly of lamb

Handful of rock salt

½ bunch of fresh thyme, chopped

1 lamb loin, trimmed up (all sinew removed)

200g faggot mix (get your butcher to do this and wrap in caul fat)

To serve:

Greens of your choice

Method

For the artichoke

Peel and chop eight of the artichokes into four thick discs. In a heavy-bottomed pan add the milk, butter and stock cube. Add the chopped artichokes and cook for 20 minutes until soft. Scoop out the artichokes and place in a blender. Blitz on full power for 3-4 minutes, adding a little bit of stock from the pan until you have a purée consistency. Add a splash of truffle oil (optional) and season. Peel and thinly slice the two remaining artichokes on a mandoline and deep-fry until crisp.

For the cannelloni

In a food processor blitz the cheese and sun-blushed tomatoes and basil, slowly adding the cream until it is a mousse-like consistency. Place in a piping bag and refrigerate.

Cook the lasagne sheets in boiling water for 2 minutes and refresh in iced water. Pat the sheets dry. Using the piping bag, pipe a generous amount of the mousse across the top width of the rectangle sheet leaving space at the edge to fold in. Then roll it up (like a spring roll, so the ends are also covered) and egg wash across the top to glue. Wrap tightly in cling film and refrigerate for 1 hour.

For the lamb

Preheat the oven to 160°c. Rub the belly with rock salt and the thyme. Place on a cooling rack with an oven tray underneath to catch the fat. Cook in the preheated oven for 4 hours, turning over every hour.

In a hot non-stick frying pan, sear the loin and wrapped faggot and colour on both sides. Cook in the oven at 180°c for 5-6 minutes, then leave to rest for a good 5 minutes.

To serve

Remove the cannelloni from the cling film, deep-fry in hot oil for 2 minutes until golden and crispy. Assemble with the lamb and purée as shown. Serve with greens of your choice… we used podded broad beans and blistered some whole spring onions. Enjoy!

Contemporary
FINE DINING

Set within the iconic mill where Colman's Mustard began life, Stoke Mill is a piece of Norfolk history which is now home to award-winning cuisine in beautiful surroundings.

There has been a mill at Stoke Holy Cross for 700 years, and it was here that Jeremiah and James Colman began making their world-famous mustard over 200 years ago. The mill was bought by the Iaccarino family in 1969 and was run as a successful high-class restaurant for over 40 years.

In September 2013, Ludovico Iaccarino took over the family business in partnership with chef Andrew Rudd. They decided to invest in the historic premises to reinvent the restaurant for modern diners. An impressive refurbishment took place. Sympathetic to the character of the mill, they restored and revealed original features and complemented the stunning space with solid oak tables and soft pastel hues.

Since it reopened, Ludo and Andy haven't had much time to reflect on the experience as they have been fully booked night after night, but they are thrilled to have been supported so strongly by the local community and have welcomed many visitors who used to frequent the restaurant many decades ago.

Thanks to social media and excellent reviews on TripAdvisor, the restaurant quickly earned a reputation as one of the top places in the county for contemporary fine dining.

Chef patron Andy Rudd uses local produce whenever he can. They love to work with organic farmers and local producers to bring the best of the region's bounty into the kitchen. A creative chef, Andy changes the menu often as he takes inspiration from the seasonal ingredients on his doorstep.

A lovely spot for Sunday lunch, Stoke Mill tends to get booked up in advance for its high-quality two or three-course menus. Afternoon tea is also popular – even more so when accompanied by a glass of Champagne.

It is perhaps the à la carte and taster menus that have really set Stoke Mill apart as a premier fine dining destination. From wild Norfolk sea bass and hand-dived scallops to Dingley Dell pork and Paddocks beef – beautiful ingredients are cooked with skill, imagination and creativity.

Stoke Mill
PAELLA WITH NORFOLK WILD SEA BASS

A medley of top-quality, fresh ingredients make this a show-stopping dish.

Preparation time: 15 minutes | Cooking time: 30 minutes | Serves 4

Ingredients

100g Norfolk Marsh Pig chorizo, sliced

1 onion, finely chopped

1 fennel bulb, finely chopped

4 garlic cloves, finely chopped

2 litres organic chicken stock, hot

2 large pinches of saffron

1 heaped tsp smoked paprika

500g paella rice

50g peas

3 plum tomatoes, chopped

2 red peppers, roasted and chopped

10 king prawns

500g mussels

2 small squid, chopped

2 fillets of Norfolk wild sea bass

1 small bunch flat-leafed parsley, leaves picked and chopped

Lemon wedges, to serve

Method

Put the pan on the heat. Add the sliced chorizo and fry until browned and crispy. Add the onion, fennel and garlic and cook until soft. Meanwhile infuse half the hot chicken stock with the saffron. Add the smoked paprika, rice and infused stock to the pan and leave to cook on medium heat, stirring from time to time.

After 20 minutes the rice should be nearly cooked. At this point, pour in the rest of the stock along with the peas, chopped tomatoes, peppers, prawns, mussels and squid. Pan fry the sea bass on both sides for 2 minutes. Finally, serve sprinkled with chopped parsley and a wedge of lemon, with the sea bass on top.

Swanning ABOUT

A real credit to Loddon, The Swan are all about championing local produce from the fantastic area around them, so pull up a seat at the bar or dine al fresco in their charming courtyard garden.

Back in 2012, Justin Fenwick purchased The Swan and then alongside business partner Andrew Freeland brought it a new lease of life. It was previously boarded up and in the words of Andrew, "in need of some 'TLC'", which it received, through extensive planning and investment.

The Swan boasts a comprehensive history as a pub, spanning over three centuries. It originally started up as a coaching house in the 1700s, and over the years it became the hub of the area. The independent freehouse has come a long way since its early days, exhibiting a relaxed bar area as well as four dining rooms including a new restaurant, beer garden and events room. You can even enjoy an overnight stay, with four boutique bedrooms and three more currently being developed.

When it comes to food, it is all about Norfolk produce here. Nearby farmers and fishermen source the freshest of ingredients to ensure the best the region has to offer is served up. The seasonal menus are curated by talented head chef Jason Wright, who is constantly refining and developing cutting edge dishes. This is with the help of Andrew's wife Joan who supplies the lamb, Heckingham Hall Farm beef and a neighbouring estate who provides them with venison.

Classic pub dishes like fish and chips have been taken up a notch but there is also a range of more technical dishes, such as duck breast served with charred onions, mousseline potato, wild mushroom and pickled blackberry, pea panna cotta and smoked salmon mousse. Not forgetting their renowned Sunday lunches and set lunch menus! Tourists, workers, walkers, shooting parties and others from further afield travel to The Swan to taste their exquisite fare so it's important to them that they maintain a modern and exciting menu that is accessible to all.

The drinks on offer are equally as important as the food, pumps are flowing with traditional local ales and there's an eclectic wine list to boot. Whether it be a pint from the Humpty Dumpty brewery at Reedham or a tall glass of Norwich Gin and tonic that tickles your fancy, you won't be left disappointed.

Manager Kelly Wright and husband Jason, along with the front of house team, dedicate themselves to making your visit as enjoyable as possible. The unique offerings The Swan provides have not gone unnoticed, as it has received a prestigious AA rosette and 4 AA stars for accommodation. In addition to this, they have been a finalist twice in the EDP pub of the year awards. We're convinced!

RACK OF TOFT MONKS LAMB, SALT-BAKED POTATOES AND SAUCE VIERGE

This recipe uses some beautiful award-winning Jacobs's sheep from our own flock. (Winner of small Jacob's sheep flock 2016 eastern region.) Our sauce vierge contains dill but any other soft herb will be fine also. Salt baking potatoes is a great way of cooking as it also seasons the potato during the cooking process.

Preparation time: 30 minutes | Cooking time: 90 minutes | Serves 2

Ingredients

For the salt-baked potatoes:

6 large egg whites

200g fine sea salt

500g new potatoes

For the sauce vierge:

2 plum tomatoes

1 banana shallot

½ garlic clove

1 lemon, juiced

50ml rapeseed oil

30g dill

For the lamb:

1 tbsp vegetable oil

6-bone rack of lamb, French trimmed

Seasoning

Method

For the salt-baked potatoes

Preheat the oven to 200°c and line a baking tray with baking parchment.

Whisk the egg whites until stiff peaks form then gently fold in the salt to create a paste that holds its shape. Put half of the mixture onto the tray and flatten to about 1cm thick. Place the potatoes onto the egg whites leaving space between the potatoes. Cover the potatoes with the remaining mix ensuring there are no gaps. Bake in the oven for 90 minutes and then leave to rest.

For the sauce vierge

Bring a pan of water to the boil. Remove the eye of the tomatoes and make a cross in the bottom before putting them into the boiling water. Leave for 10 seconds before removing and placing them straight into iced water.

When cool remove the skin of the tomatoes, quarter and remove the seeds. Dice the flesh of the tomatoes and place in a small saucepan. Finely dice the shallot and garlic and add to the pan along with the lemon juice and oil. Roughly chop the dill, mix in and allow to infuse.

For the lamb

Heat the vegetable oil in a non-stick pan. Season the lamb all over and place carefully in the pan skin side down. Cook on a medium heat for 2 minutes and then place the pan into the oven for 8 minutes. Turn the lamb over and allow to rest in the pan in a warm place for 4 minutes.

To serve

Gently warm the sauce on a low heat for 1 minute. Carefully crack the salt crust and remove the potatoes. Cut the lamb in-between each bone and serve.

Working
TOGETHER

The beautiful Thornage Hall Estate is home to a unique supported living environment where people with learning disabilities can live, learn and work together in a meaningful and sustainable way.

Thornage Hall's mission is based on the belief that everyone has something to learn and everyone has something to give. It is a community based in the picturesque rural setting of the Norfolk Countryside, which is centred around a biodynamic farm.

A unique approach to supported living, Thornage Hall is a member of the Association of Camphill Communities and it was established in 1989. As such it recognises the individual contributions of each and every member of the community by seeking to respect, value and enhance the strengths and potential of everyone supporting them to be the person they want to be.

The biodynamic farm is intrinsic to these founding principles. It provides a range of work opportunities for tenants as well those coming in from the surrounding area. In this respect, it is quite unusual from many other supported living establishments as it can provide a rural way of life that is rarely available for adults with learning disabilities. Working on the farm can mean many different roles, it is not only the animals and seven acres of crops that need care, but also the environmental management of the estate. They are constantly striving to increase the biodiversity of the farm to create the perfect ecosystems.

The farm produces food for everyone living at Thornage Hall, but they also produce plenty more too. The surplus is much sought-after in the region and they have developed a strong relationship with esteemed chef Galton Blackiston and supply his Michelin-starred restaurant Morston Hall, as well as Richard Bainbridge's Benedicts.

Alongside a medley of impressive art and craft workshops, Thornage Hall also houses cookery workshops where tenants can learn to transform their home-grown produce into delicious dishes. And with an onsite bakery too, there is no end to the potential for homemade meals. Thornage Hall certainly celebrates the farm-to-fork philosophy!

Having an essential role makes each and every member of the community intrinsically valuable. It not only provides a sense of purpose but also the satisfaction of having a positive impact on the local environment. Whether cook, baker, gardener, farmer, woodworker or artist, every member of this diverse community can enjoy the benefits of sustainable living – and the rest of Norfolk can enjoy the beautiful food and crafts they produce.

Thornage Hall

RED POLL FILLET STEAK, CHERRY TOMATO & CUMIN SAUCE, PURPLE BROCCOLI, SQUASH & ALMOND CAKES

The Red Poll beef from the Thornage Hall farm is simply sensational. It has been grown bio-dynamically and nurtured to the highest possible standards and the results are so good! This recipe has been inspired by the produce grown here and represents just a few of the many fruit and vegetables carefully grown from seed to harvest.

Preparation time: 20 minutes | Cooking time: 40 minutes | Serves 2

Ingredients

For the cherry tomato and toasted cumin sauce:

5g cumin seeds

20g butter

50g onion, chopped

1 clove garlic

10g brown sugar

20g tomato purée

20ml white wine vinegar

200g cherry tomatoes, halved

50ml chicken stock

For the squash and almond cakes:

150g squash, peeled and diced

Olive oil, for drizzling

150g potato, peeled and chopped

20g coriander, chopped

50g plain flour

1 egg, beaten

100g flaked almonds

20ml sunflower oil

For the steaks and to serve:

2 x 150g Thornage Hall Red Poll fillet steaks

200g purple sprouting broccoli

Salt and pepper

Method

For the cherry tomato and toasted cumin sauce

In a dry frying pan toast the cumin seeds over a high heat until the seeds begin to release their aroma, then remove from the pan and grind down in a pestle and mortar. Set aside. In a saucepan melt the butter and gently sauté the onion and garlic until soft. Add the brown sugar and tomato purée and then caramelise the onion and garlic. Add the vinegar to deglaze. When the vinegar has evaporated, add the halved cherry tomatoes and the chicken stock, then reduce by half the volume. Add the ground toasted cumin. The sauce can now be puréed with a stick blender and set aside.

For the squash and almond cakes

Preheat the oven to 180°c. Roast the squash in the preheated oven with a drizzle of olive oil for 20 minutes until soft. Meanwhile boil the potatoes until just soft then strain and crush with a fork.

Add the squash and coriander to the crushed potato, mix together then allow to cool.

When the potato and squash mixture is cool, shape four cakes of equal size with your hands. Put the flour in one bowl, the beaten egg in another bowl and the flaked almonds in a third. Coat the cakes first in the flour, then dip them in the egg, then roll the cakes around in the flaked almonds.

To cook the potato and almond cakes, warm a frying pan with some sunflower oil and fry them for 1 minute on each side, then put in the oven for 5 minutes while you assemble the rest of the dish.

To serve

In the same frying pan you used for the cakes, fry the steaks for 1 minute on each side, remove them from the pan then season with salt and pepper.

Add the purple sprouting broccoli to salted boiling water for 30 seconds then strain.

To assemble, put a spoonful of tomato sauce on a plate and spread with back of a spoon, place the cakes next to the sauce then place the steak and purple sprouting broccoli next to each other in the space left on the plate.

Beautifully BOUTIQUE

Family-run hotel and restaurant Titchwell Manor has all the charm of a small family business alongside national recognition for culinary excellence.

Titchwell Manor has been part of the Snaith family for 29 years, since Margaret and Ian Snaith bought the old Victorian farmhouse and transformed it into a boutique hotel overlooking the open marshes and the Norfolk coast.

Being a family business means that Titchwell Manor has retained a certain quirkiness and charm that comes from keeping family values at its heart. It has evolved organically over the last three decades as the Snaiths have reinvested in the business and built it up gradually to become the award-winning destination it is today.

Margaret and Ian's son Eric, who was head chef for 12 years, has recently taken the reins from his parents and appointed Chris Mann as head chef. Eric Snaith has earned a reputation for culinary excellence through innovative techniques and the use of interesting local ingredients. Chris had worked with Eric for eight years before taking the role of head chef, and he continues to shape the modern European cooking for which the hotel has become known.

Having worked with many regional suppliers for decades, Eric has developed enviable relationships with some of Norfolk's most sought-after producers. From Brancaster mussels and freshly caught crab to Norfolk quail and Houghton venison, the county is served up on a plate. You will even find unusual touches such as foraged marsh vegetables in the accomplished cooking here.

The menus of both The Eating Rooms and Conservatory Restaurant reflect the hotel's location on the Norfolk coast with a balance between fish and seafood from the coastline and meat, vegetables and seasonal game from the land.

There is also a balance between classic dishes – think fish pie, perfect steaks or Eric's famous fish and chips – and creative contemporary cooking, which has earned them three AA rosettes, putting them amongst the top restaurants in the UK. Although Titchwell Manor has become a firm favourite for special occasions or family celebrations, it is also somewhere to enjoy a relaxed dinner, afternoon tea or Sunday roast.

If you take advantage of one of the 26 beautifully appointed boutique hotel rooms, you can also sample the renowned Titchwell Manor breakfast, too.

CHARRED MACKEREL WITH APPLE, GOLDEN TURNIP AND DRIED DILL

The apple vinegar needs to be started at least 10 hours in advance, as it requires lengthy dehydrating and infusing times, but this can be made up to a month ahead.

Preparation time: 1 hour, plus 45 minutes brining and 4 hours infusing | Cooking time: 6 hours | Serves 4

Ingredients

For the mackerel:

100g salt

100g sugar

4 large mackerel fillets

For the dried dill:

1 bunch of dill

For the apple vinegar:

4 apples

150g cider vinegar

150g chardonnay vinegar

20g sugar

For the dill oil:

1 bunch dill

300g grapeseed oil

For the turnips:

3 golden turnips

300ml water

3 tbsp sugar

½ tbsp salt

To finish:

2 Granny Smith apples, diced into 5mm squares

½ lemon, juiced

Method

For the mackerel

Mix the salt and sugar together and completely cover the mackerel fillets underneath and on top. Leave to brine for 45 minutes. Thoroughly wash and pat dry, then cut the fillets in half lengthways either side of the bones.

For the dried dill

Pick the dill and lay onto a tray. Reserve the stalks and set aside. Place the dill in a dehydrator or a very low oven (around 50°c) until completely dry, this should only take a couple of hours.

For the apple vinegar

Quarter the apples leaving the skin and core intact, and then dehydrate in the oven until dry, this will probably take a bit longer, around 6 hours. Place the dried apples in a pan along with the vinegars and sugar, and bring to the boil. Cover with cling film and turn down until it just stays warm, then leave this to infuse for 4 hours. The apple vinegar can then be stored like this for up to a month in a fridge so can be made way in advance, and kept for multiple uses.

For the dill oil

Combine the dill with the stalks left over from the dried dill, and roughly chop. Cover with the oil and blend. Pass through a muslin and keep chilled to retain its colour.

For the turnips

Neatly dice the turnip into roughly 5mm dices and place in a pan with the water, salt and sugar. Bring to the boil, then remove from the heat and allow to cool.

To finish

Place the cooked turnip into a bowl along with the diced apple. Add a small squeeze of lemon juice, 12 tbsp of dill oil and 8 tbsp of the apple vinegar, mix everything together. Then either using a blowtorch or a very hot grill, char the mackerel on the skin-side only; the flesh-side should remain semi-raw as the apple vinegar will continue to cook it once it is on the plate.

Divide the apple and turnip equally amongst four plates, then place one fillet of mackerel (two pieces) on to each plate. Pour over the dill oil/apple vinegar dressing, dividing it equally amongst all the plates. Finally finish with plenty of the dried dill on top.

Vocal about LOCAL

Connecting local producers directly with customers, this is a farm shop that caters for all your needs and more.

When Walsingham Farms Shop was set up, it was as a partnership to help local farmers and food producers get their produce straight to the customer, bypassing wholesalers and minimising food miles. A special focus is on grass fed beef produced by partner James Woodhouse at Hill House Farm, Walsingham. As well as the original shop in the centre of historic Walsingham, the partnership has a second outlet at Norfolk Lavender in Heacham. Both are housed in beautiful converted barns and filled with all manner of locally sourced goodies.

Their vision is to celebrate everything that is great about Norfolk food, whether that's through locally sourced ingredients to cook with, or treats they have whipped up in their open kitchen. Scouting locally is first and foremost but for the right quality, they will widen their circle. Candi's Chutney, Cley Smokehouse, Mrs Temple's Cheese, Norfolk Saffron, Winbirri Vineyards and The Norfolk Sloe Company are just a few of many producers they work with and they don't haggle with them as it's important to the local economy - at least 75% of their range comes from within Norfolk and 95% within the UK.

You can be sure that anything with the Walsingham label on it has been cooked or prepared in their own kitchens – expect everything from pies, sausage rolls, pasties and stews to cakes, tarts and desserts. The contemporary food emporium also supplies local restaurants and gastro-pubs with their pies and meat, including the Black Lion in Walsingham, the Golden Fleece in Wells, and of course the Norfolk Lavender café right next to their Heacham shop.

Understanding the provenance of what they sell is of utmost importance. James Woodhouse's Aberdeen sired, grass fed, suckler herd can be seen grazing on nearby meadows, and the beef is exclusive to Walsingham Farms Shop. As farmers, they would love their customers to understand more about how food is produced locally and how the countryside is shaped by food production. They do this through Open Farm Sunday, local farmer's markets and county shows, but ultimately through stocking hyperlocal and seasonal produce.

Doing what they do has bagged them an EDP Norfolk Food & Drink award for Best Independent Food & Drink Retailer previously and they were finalists in 2016. "It is not just a shop that happens to be on a farm. We embrace the theatre of shopping. Being here should be a pleasurable, fun experience whether you are watching sausages or game pies being made, learning about food production or tasting something from a nearby producer. Shopping with us is experiencing Norfolk food," says partner Elizabeth Meath Baker.

Norfolk made

Mince Beef &
Onion Pie

lean local minced beef with caramelised onions in
a rich beef gravy

• Free Range Beef · Mill House
Farm · Walsingham

Contains:
Wheat Gluten, Milk, Egg

£2.95 Small
£9.95 Large

Belly Pork Slices
£6.50/kg

Walsingham Farms Shop

· CELEBRATING · NORFOLK ·
· FOOD ·

Walsingham

Walsingham Farms Shop

MINCED BEEF AND BINHAM BLUE CHEESE PIE

At Walsingham Farms Shop we pride ourselves in the local produce we sell and especially the products we make in our delis. Our most popular product we make is by far our range of innovative meat and vegetable pies. We can produce hundreds a week all homemade and hand-finished with a signature garnish. This recipe is a favourite of ours as it uses minced beef from our herd of Aberdeen Angus cross cattle reared on the Walsingham Estate, blended with our favourite local cheese – Mrs Temple's Binham Blue cheese.

Preparation time: 1 hour | Cooking time: 30-60 minutes | Serves 4

Ingredients

For the pastry:

90ml water

75g butter

75g lard

¼ tsp salt

300g plain Norfolk flour

Egg wash

For the filling:

250g Hill House Farm beef mince

20ml Norfolk rapeseed oil

120g onions, finely sliced

120g mushrooms

20g beef bouillon

50ml water

15g cornflour

20ml Longley Farm double cream

Cracked black pepper

30g Binham Blue Cheese

Method

For the pastry

First boil the water, butter, lard and salt until all the fats have melted. Then combine it with the flour in a mixer.

Leave the pastry to cool but do not chill.

For the filling

Brown the beef mince in batches using the rapeseed oil and reserve in a dish.

Fry the onions and mushrooms in the same pan, then mix the beef bouillon in 25ml of water and add to vegetables before adding the mince back to the pan. Simmer for 5 minutes.

Mix the rest of the water and the cornflour into the beef mix and heat until thick and bubbling. Remove from the heat and add the cream and Binham Blue cheese - stir until well combined.

To assemble

Preheat the oven to 180°c.

Flour a work surface and roll out two-thirds of the pastry to 3-4 mm thickness. Line your pie tins with the pastry and roll out the remaining pastry for the lids – cut to the correct size.

Once the beef mixture has cooled, fill the pie moulds and top with the pie lids. Crimp the edges with a fork, egg wash and make a small hole in the middle.

Garnish as you wish although a little sprinkle of cracked black pepper is always a nice touch!

Cook for 30-40 minutes if making four small pies. For one large pie cook 45 minutes to an hour or until the pastry is golden and crisp.

Quite a CATCH

With a beautiful setting in one of Norfolk's picturesque fishing towns, Wells Crab House is in the perfect place to enjoy the freshest seafood... straight from the boat to the plate.

Wells-next-the-Sea enjoys an enviable location on the North Norfolk coast. A bustling seaside town during the summer, it is also a popular spot year-round thanks to the outstanding natural beauty of the landscape. At the heart of the town is Wells Crab House, which reopened with its new name in 2016 following a refurbishment by owners Kelly and Scott.

The husband and wife team have many years of experience in the hospitality industry, and their passion for food and customer service has helped them to make Wells Crab House one of the area's most popular dining spots. Families with kids are welcome earlier in the evening, while 7:30pm onwards is reserved for adults and older children.

Using local seafood is top-priority for Kelly and Scott – and when they have access to such incredible fresh fish, you can see why. They source crabs and mussels from Frary's, lobsters from Billy Ward and oysters from Richard Loose, and of course they do also serve some 'landlubber' too, which they source from award-winning butcher Arthur Howell.

The bright and light feel from the pale blue décor is complemented by the rustic wooden tables, and there are a few intriguing ocean-related knickknacks dotted about that create the ideal ambience for tucking into freshly caught seafood.

Part of the excitement with freshly caught seafood is never quite knowing what will be available each day, and this allows the chefs to be inventive with their menus. The specials board changes daily depending on what is in season, and flavouring inspiration comes from all around the globe.

From Norfolk mussels mariniere with bloomer bread to tempura king prawns with hot homemade sweet chilli dip and pickled ginger shreds the starters are all designed to get the tastebuds tingling. For 'the main catch' it can be a struggle to choose between Frary's dressed Wells crab or Billy Ward's steamed half lobster... so you can opt for a combination of both, if you like. Other dishes include delights such as skate, hake or turbot, which are cooked to perfection by the skilled chefs.

Wells Crab House
CRAB NEWBURG

Make the pickle a day or two in advance, as it will improve once left in the fridge.

Preparation time: 1 hour, plus salting and steeping | Cooking time: 20 minutes | Serves 6

Ingredients

For the pickle:

6 cucumbers

500ml of vinegar mixed with 500ml of water and 200g of caster sugar (I do it by eye, so try 100g sugar first and then add the other 100g if you find it too sharp, or more, to taste)

Spices of choice

1 onion or 3 shallots

2 sticks of celery

½ bulb fennel

Salt

Bunch of dill, finely chopped

For the crab:

6 large "Jack" crabs, cleaned, boiled and allowed to cool (ask your fishmonger to do this, or we get ours from Andy Frary's stall on Wells Quay)

250ml double cream

250ml milk

2 tsp smoked paprika

3 tsp English mustard powder

100g butter

100g plain flour

50ml brandy

100ml dry sherry

2 eggs, beaten

A handful of lovage, chopped

200g goat's cheese, crumbled

Method

For the pickle

To salt the cucumbers, slice them as thin as you can (1.5mm is ideal, but tough without a mandoline). Put them in a colander and mix them with a really big handful of salt; don't worry about saltiness as you will rinse it off later. Leave them to drip into a sink for half an hour, or more.

Make the liquor. Mix the sugar, water and vinegar, then add whole spices – we use cinnamon (2 sticks) mustard seed (1 tbsp) coriander seeds (2 tbsp) fennel seeds (2 tbsp) star anise (5) caraway seeds (½ tbsp) bay (2 leaves) and black peppercorns (2 tbsp). Bring to the boil, then leave it to steep. While the vinegar is infusing cut the other ingredients into very thin strips and place into the pot you want to make your pickle in.

Rinse your cucumbers thoroughly but gently to remove all the salt. Drain and, if possible, blot dry on a tea towel. Add them to the shredded vegetables. Bring the liquor back to the boil and strain it onto the soon-to-be pickles. Cover the top with cling film or baking paper and leave to cool. Once cool, mix in the dill and refrigerate. Leave it overnight or for a couple of days if possible.

For the crab

Prepare the crab. (If you don't want to do this part you can buy crab meat and use gratin dishes.) Split the shell away from the body. Remove the large front claws and reserve, discarding the body and small legs. Remove the dead man's fingers (gills) from the shell, and remove the face by pushing down gently into the shell until it cracks, ensuring there is no bone left behind. Scrape all the shell meat into a bowl, and place the empty shell into boiling water to clean. Using a rolling pin, crack the reserved claws, then using a pick, remove every bit of meat, ensuring you don't collect any of the bony white "feathers". Add this meat to the shell meat and set aside.

Preheat the oven to 180°c. Warm the cream, milk, paprika and mustard in a pan and keep on a low heat so it doesn't boil.

In a large pan, melt the butter with a dash of oil (to stop the butter burning). Remove from the heat, add the flour and whisk to a smooth paste. Return to a low heat and cook for 2-3 minutes, stirring constantly to avoid any lumps forming. Remove from the heat and add the warm cream mixture, brandy, sherry, eggs and lovage. Whisk until thick. Stir in the crab meat and season with salt and pepper to taste.

Take the crab shells out of the boiling water, ensuring they are clean (you may need to scrape the inside). Wipe dry. Spoon the Newburg mixture into the shells. Sprinkle with the goat's cheese crumbs. Place on a baking tray and bake in the preheated oven for 15 minutes or until the cheese has melted. Place under a hot grill for a few minutes to brown.

Serve with a crisp dressed salad, hot buttered new potatoes and the pickle.

Gallop away
AND ESCAPE

Perfectly situated up from Blakeney Quay on the stunning North Norfolk coast, The White Horse is just as a modern pub should be – welcoming and characterful with a hint of style.

Popular with the local crowd, The White Horse has always been a go-to place, whether it's just for a couple of drinks, or dinner and the full works. Its great location, coupled with a warm and informal atmosphere, a well-kept range of award-winning Adnams beers, spirits and wines, and great food, entices people from far and wide.

The chefs have good relationships with local farmers and fishermen to ensure their produce is the best quality it can be, sustainable and right for the season. At The White Horse, you are truly spoilt for choice when perusing the inviting menu, where you'll find reassuring coastal classics, as well as lesser-expected dishes to indulge in. Choose from the ultimate comfort food such as Ghost Ship beer-battered cod and chips, fish pie using produce from the local smokehouse, as well as local pork tenderloin to tantalise the taste buds. Local ingredients are a given at the White Horse, and some of their favourite producers include the Cley Smokehouse, Perfick Pork at Gt. Ryburgh and Mrs Temple's cheeses at Wighton.

The White Horse is part of a small coastal collective of quality Adnams pubs and inns. Hence, it showcases an impressive range of well-kept Adnams' beers, wines and spirits; they even use these in their recipes to jazz things up and offer customers something a little different. The White Horse team work closely with the Adnams brewery, distillery and wine buying team to create interesting events in the pub, including craft beer nights, aswell as spirits and wine tastings. The White Horse also supports local events and is actively involved in 'Norfolk Food & Drink'. "It's important for us to be part of the Blakeney community and also promote Norfolk's outstanding food and drink further afield," says general manager, Tom Pickard.

The White Horse team try and think of everything to make your North Norfolk experience the best it can be, with daily tide times on display, plus wellies and binoculars available to hire (in case you've left yours at home). The pub welcomes all sorts, including the furry, four-legged fraternity with homemade dog biscuits, a dog watering station and lots of space for them to run around including the courtyard at the back of the pub.

The recent admittance into the Michelin Guide 2017 is testament that the White Horse really is a 'must visit' in North Norfolk!

PORK BELLY AND CHEEK WITH BLACK PUDDING, BUTTER BEANS AND APPLE PURÉE

This is a bestseller on our specials menu and it showcases one of our favourite local producers, Perfick Pork. It's also two dishes in one – a real dinner party winner. It's best to prepare the pork cheeks a day in advance.

Preparation time: 45 minutes plus 1 hour salting | Cooking time: 4 – 4 ½ hours | Serves 6

Ingredients

6 trimmed pork cheeks

2 carrots, diced

2 shallots, diced

1 bay leaf

1 star anise

200ml Sandringham apple juice

400ml chicken stock

1kg trimmed boneless pork belly

Flour

1 egg

Fine breadcrumbs

4 Braeburn apples

½ lemon, juiced

Sunflower oil

150g black pudding, diced

150g butter beans, cooked

Splash of Adnams Pomme Pom

500g curly kale

Method

Season and brown the pork cheeks in a deep pan before adding the carrots, shallots, bay leaf and star anise. Cook gently without further colouring for 5 minutes.

Add the apple juice and stock, bring to the boil, and then tightly cover the pan with a lid. Simmer for 3-4 hours on a gentle heat.

When cooked, remove the star anise and bay leaf, and refrigerate the cheeks in the cooking liquor overnight.

Rub a little sea salt into the pork belly skin. Leave for 1 hour. This will help draw excess moisture from the skin and produce a crispier skin.

Preheat the oven to 150°c.

Slow roast the pork belly in the oven for about 4 hours until soft and tender. When the pork is nearly cooked, raise the heat to 180°c for about 15 minutes to crisp the skin off.

While the pork is cooking, remove the pork cheeks from the cooking liquor. Pat dry, dust with flour, dip in beaten egg and then toss in breadcrumbs. Repeat the process twice for a good coating.

Bring the cooking liquor back to the boil and gently reduce until it starts to thicken.

To make the apple purée, core the apples and roughly chop (you can leave the skin on). Put in a pan with lemon juice, cover with a tight fitting lid and cook for about 8 minutes or until soft. Purée the mixture in a food processor then strain through a fine sieve. Keep purée warm on the side.

Fry the pork cheeks in sunflower oil until lightly coloured. Finish in the oven for 10 minutes at 180°c with the pork belly.

Quickly flash-fry the black pudding in a pan, drain off any oil and add the pudding to the reduced cooking liquor with the butter beans. Add a splash of Adnams Pomme Pom when nearly ready to serve.

Cook the kale in a little boiling buttered water, drain off and keep warm.

To serve

Carve the pork into six neat blocks. Set on top of the kale, spoon some of the butter bean stew to the side of the pork belly and place a cheek on top. Finish with a spoon of apple purée.

Award-winning BREWERY

For over 35 years, Woodforde's Brewery have been taking simple ingredients and transforming them into great-tasting beer.

Woodforde's is close to the hearts of the people of Norfolk as the largest regional brewer in the county. It is named after Parson Woodforde, an 18th-century Norfolk clergyman whose diaries reveal an epicurean passion for good food and good ale – in fact he often brewed ale himself.

The brewery was established in 1981 by two members of the Norwich Homebrewers' Society. The first brew was the famous Wherry Bitter and today the brewery still follows the exact same recipe using just four ingredients. They celebrate the provenance of these ingredients – including water from their own bore hole and Norfolk-grown barley – and the resulting unique local heritage.

Over the years, they have achieved a plethora of awards, including the coveted CAMRA Supreme Champion Beer of Britain for their Wherry Bitter.

The emphasis is on producing an eclectic range of great-tasting beers, and this comes down to the simplicity of using excellent ingredients and celebrating the extraordinary flavour of real ales. Master brewer Belinda Jennings, one of the country's leading female brewers, has played an important role in keeping this integrity at the heart of the company while nurturing innovation and leading Woodforde's into exciting new times.

People can come and visit the state of the art brewery to see for themselves how Woodforde's are making their innovative beers. The brewery tours are very popular, even more so when combined with a visit to the brewery tap, The Fur & Feather, where the full range of beers is available.

Beer and food go hand-in-hand, and head chef Tim Abbott combines great beer and great food at The Fur & Feather in all sorts of ways. Woodforde's beers are used to add flavour to many of its hearty dishes and the pub often hosts beer and food matching events.

With its picturesque location near the Norfolk Broads, Woodforde's and their brewery tap, The Fur & Feather, is a destination centre for visitors to the area, as well as a favourite for locals.

Woodforde's
SLOW-COOKED BEEF CHEEKS IN WOODFORDE'S PORTER

Hearty slow-cooked beef cheeks are served with roasted garlic mash, honey and cumin roasted heritage carrots, kale and gremolata. The beef cheeks need to be marinated for at least 12 hours, so start this the day before.

Preparation time: 15 minutes | Cooking time: 40 minutes | Serves 4

Ingredients

For the beef cheeks:

4 large beef cheeks

2 onions, roughly chopped

1 carrot, cut into chunks

1 bulb garlic, cut in half

3 sprigs thyme

2 x 500ml bottle Woodforde's porter beer

2 tbsp olive oil

150g butter

750ml beef stock

Salt and freshly ground black pepper

For the carrots:

1kg heritage carrots

2 star anise

100g butter

50g honey

2 tsp cumin

Salt and freshly ground black pepper

For the mash:

1kg floury potatoes, peeled and cut into chunks

150g butter

150ml full-fat milk or cream

½ bulb garlic, blanched in milk and roasted

Salt and freshly ground black pepper

For the gremolata:

Bunch of parsley, finely chopped

1 red onion, finely diced

1 lemon, zest

1 tsp capers

1 clove of garlic, finely grated

Method

For the beef cheeks

Place the cheeks in a large bowl with the onions, carrot, garlic and thyme. Pour over the beer, cover and place in the fridge for at least 12 hours, but preferably overnight.

Preheat the oven to 150°c/300°F/Gas 2. Lift the beef cheeks out from the vegetables, pat dry, then season with salt and pepper. Reserve the marinade. Heat a large casserole or ovenproof pan until hot, add the olive oil and a knob of the butter. When foaming, add the beef cheeks two at a time and fry on each side until browned. Remove and set aside.

Return the beef to the pan with the reserved marinade and add the beef stock. Bring to a simmer then cover with a lid, leaving the lid slightly ajar so you have a 1cm/½in gap at the side. Cook in the oven for 4-5 hours.

For the carrots

Meanwhile, put the whole carrots, star anise, butter, honey, cumin, salt and pepper, wrapped in tin foil and roast for 20-30 minutes, or until the carrots are tender and glazed.

Back to the beef cheeks

Remove the casserole from the oven and strain the sauce into a saucepan, then place over the heat and cook until the volume of liquid has reduced and is thick enough to just coat the back of a spoon. Whisk in the remaining butter until the sauce is shiny. Season with sea salt and freshly ground black pepper, to taste.

For the mash

Place the potatoes into a pan of cold, salted water and bring to the boil. Reduce the heat and simmer for 12-15 minutes, or until the potatoes are tender. Drain and return to the pan, then place over a low heat for a couple of minutes to dry the potatoes slightly. Meanwhile, put the butter and milk or cream into a saucepan and simmer until the butter is melted, add the roasted garlic. Pass the potatoes through a ricer, then add the hot butter and milk mixture, and beat to form a very smooth mash. Season to taste with salt and black pepper.

For the gremolata

Mix the ingredients together.

To serve

Lift out the beef cheeks and place in shallow bowls. Spoon the mash and carrots alongside and finish with a generous ladleful of sauce and a good spoonful of gremolata.

The DIRECTORY

These great businesses have supported the making of this book; please support and enjoy them.

A Passion to Inspire
Murray Chapman MCGB Master CGC
First Contact Chefs
Telephone: 0114 245 8696
Email: murray@firstcontactuk.com
Non-profit-making initiative that works with colleges, farms and top chefs to inspire, encourage and support students in their chosen careers.

Archer's Butchers
177-179 Plumstead Road,
Norwich
Norfolk NR1 4AB
Telephone: 01603 434253
Website: www.archersbutchers.com
Award-winning family run butchery specialising in high-quality local breeds.

Back to the Garden
Fakenham Road
Letheringsett
Norfolk NR25 7JJ
Telephone: 01263 715996
Website:
www.back-to-the-garden.co.uk
A multi award-winning farm shop, butcher, deli & cafe, whose aim is to produce the very best local, fresh and traceable food.

Benedicts
9 St Benedicts Street,
Norwich
Norfolk, NR2 4PE
Telephone: 01603 926 080
Website: www.restaurantbenedicts.com
Benedicts is a contemporary bistro with classic values, serving modern sophisticated food in a relaxed environment.

The Bicycle Shop
17 St Benedicts Street
Norwich
Norfolk NR2 4PE
Telephone: 01603 625777
Website: www.bicycleshopcafe.com
From the first breakfast to the last cocktail, The Bicycle Shop is here for you. But we don't sell bicycles, sorry.

Biddy's Tea Room
15a Lower Goat Lane
Norwich
Norfolk NR2 1EL

Biddy's Kitchen
16 Market Place
Aylsham NR11 6EH
Email: bookings@biddystearoom.com
Website: www.biddytsearoom.com
Vintage inspired tea room, afternoon tea specialising in loose leaf tea and homemade cake served in a charming and quirky atmosphere.

The Boars
Spooner Row
Wymondham
Norfolk NR18 9LL
Telephone: 01953 605851
Website: www.theboars.co.uk
Freehouse and restaurant. Craft beers, great food, fine wines.

Brasted's
Manor Farm Barns
Framingham Pigot
Norfolk NR14 7PZ
Telephone: 01508 491112
Website: www.brasteds.co.uk
Brasted's is a multi award-winning catering and events company, with over 30 years' experience serving royalty, dignitaries, celebrities and guests across Norfolk.

Briarfields
Main Street
Titchwell, Hunstanton
Norfolk PE31 8BB
Telephone: 01485 210742
Website:
www.briarfieldshotelnorfolk.co.uk
Located at the heart of the peaceful north-west Norfolk coastline near to Hunstanton, Briarfields at Titchwell is a hidden gem. Enjoy our tranquil setting and warm welcome.

Byfords
1-3 Shirehall Plain
Holt
Norfolk NR25 6BG
Telephone: 01263 711400
Website: www.byfords.org.uk
A higgledy piggledy world of pleasure! We're a café, store and posh B&B in Holt, Norfolk.

City College Norwich,

Ipswich Road,
Norwich NR2 2LJ
Telephone: 01603 773311
Website: www.ccn.ac.uk

Debut Restaurant

City College Norwich
Ipswich Road,
Norwich NR2 2LJ
Telephone: 01603 773227
Website:
www.debut.ccn.ac.uk/debut-restaurant
*Run by our internationally renowned
Hotel School, everyone can enjoy fabulous
food prepared and presented by the stars of
tomorrow.*

Cley Windmill

Cley-next-the-Sea
Holt
Norfolk NR25 7RP
Telephone: 01263 740209
Website: www.cleywindmill.co.uk
*"One of the most memorable and
enchanting places to stay in Britain" -
Fiona Duncan, The Telegraph*

Coxfords Butchers

11 Market Place
Aylsham
Norwich
Norfolk NR11 6EH
Telephone: 01263 732280
Website: www.coxfordsbutchers.co.uk
*Jason and Johnny are proud to source
all meats as locally as possible while
making sure it is of the highest standard.
Traditional butchery with a modern twist.*

Creake Abbey

North Creake
Fakenham
Norfolk
NorfolkNR21 9LF
Telephone: 01328 730399
Website: www.creakeabbey.co.uk
*A hidden gem comprising ancient abbey
ruins, boutique shops, services, and a
café & food hall stocking local delicacies,
all situated in a tranquil valley just a 5
minute drive from Burnham Market on
the popular north Norfolk coast.*

The Dabbling Duck

11 Abbey Road
Great Massingham
Norfolk PE32 2HN
Telephone: 01485 520827
Website: www.thedabblingduck.co.uk
*Gastropub with nine luxurious bedrooms,
great service and pub food at its best.*

The Duck Inn

Burnham Road
Stanhoe
King's Lynn
Norfolk
PE31 8QD
Telephone: 01485 518330
Website: www.duckinn.co.uk
*Award-winning Gastropub specialising
in combining global flavours with the best
locally-sourced produce. Accomodation
available.*

Eastgate Larder Ltd

Eastgate House, Easton Way
Eastgate
Norfolk NR10 4HF
Telephone: 07778 160063 / 01603
871109
Website: www.eastgatelarder.co.uk
*Norfolk's specialist grower and producer of
medlar fruit preserves.*

Figbar

23 St John Maddermarket
Norwich
Norfolk NR2 1DN
Email: hello@figbarnorwich.com
Website: www.figbarnorwich.com
*Figbar aims to amplify your sweet tooth
serving only plated desserts and sweet
treats by Michelin-trained chef Jaime
Garbutt alongside fine wines and coffee.*

The Fur & Feather Inn

Woodbastwick
Norfolk NR13 6SW
Telephone: 01603 720003
Website:
www.thefurandfeatherinn.co.uk
*Woodforde's brewery tap, home of
Woodforde's real ales.*

Garden Café

Cathedral of St John the Baptist
Earlham Road
Norwich
Norfolk NR2 3RB
Telephone: 01603 624615
Website: www.sjbcathedral.org.uk
*We serve hot and cold drinks, wholesome
food and sweet treats regardless of your
faith, beliefs or denomination.*

The Garden Pantry

3 Bunwell Road
Spooner Row
Norfolk NR18 9LH
Telephone: 01953 600011 /
07814 511374
Website: www.thegardenpantry.co.uk
*Multi-award-winning artisan jams,
chutneys and sauces, made using home-
grown and locally sourced produce.*

The Georgian Townhouse

30-34 Unthank Road
Norwich
Norfolk NR2 2RB
Telephone: 01603 615655
Website: www.
thegeorgiantownhousenorwich.com
*At The Georgian Townhouse we've created
a hidden city oasis where you can come to
escape the hustle and bustle of everyday life.*

Green Pastures Plant Centre, Farm Shop & Restaurant

Mill Road, Bergh Apton
Norwich
Norfolk NR15 1BQ
Telephone: 01508 480734
Website:
www.greenpasturesnursery.co.uk
*Multi-award-winning garden centre and
farm shop incorporating the "Gardeners
Kitchen" restaurant, growing, selling and
serving homegrown and local produce.*

The Grove, Cromer

95 Overstrand Road,
Cromer,
Norfolk NR27 0DJ
Telephone: 01263 512412
Website: www.thegrovecromer.co.uk
*Rosette-winning family-run restaurant
whose emphasis is on inventive use of local
and seasonal produce to create succulent,
flavoursome dishes. Accommodation
available.*

The Honingham Buck
29 The Street
Honingham
Norwich
Norfolk NR9 5BL
Telephone: 01603 880393
Website:
www.thehoninghambuck.co.uk
Welcoming pub serving food made from the best local produce for enjoying with friends, family, or colleagues. Accommodation available.

Lakenham Creamery Ltd
2 Trafalgar Street
Norwich
Norfolk NR1 3HN
Telephone: 01603 620970
Website: www.lakenhamcreamery.co.uk
Specialist Ice Cream makers established in 1921. Producers of Norfolk County and Aldous Range of Ice Creams. Winners of over 120 awards including 28 Great Taste Awards.

The Last Wine Bar & Restaurant
70-76 St George's Street
Norwich NR3 1AB
Telephone: 01603 626626
Website: www.lastwinebar.co.uk
A Norwich institution, 'The Last' opened its doors in 1990, and offers a warm personal welcome, a distinctive atmosphere, classic and innovative cooking, and an extensive wine list.

The Loddon Swan Ltd
23 Church Plain
Loddon
Norfolk NR34 0EJ
Telephone: 01508 528039
Website: www.theloddonswan.co.uk
Great pub with great food!

The Lodge
Old Hunstanton Road
Old Hunstanton
Norfolk PE36 6HX
Telephone: 01485 532896
Website:
www.thelodgehunstanton.co.uk
Nestled in the heart of the old village, The Lodge in Old Hunstanton Norfolk is a pub which offers a relaxed and casual experience – perfectly combining traditional and contemporary.

Moorish Falafel Bar
17 Lower Goat Lane
Norwich
Norfolk NR2 1EL
Telephone: 01603 622250
Website: www.moorishfalafelbar.com
Inspired by the zesty flavours of Mediterranean and Middle Eastern cuisine we serve fresh vegetarian and vegan food.

Morston Hall Hotel
The Street
Holt
Norfolk NR25 7AA
Telephone: 01263 741041
Website: www.morstonhall.com
Morston Hall is an intimate country house hotel with a Michelin-star restaurant.

Mustard Coffee Bar
3 Bridewell Alley
Norwich NR21AQ

Mustard Coffee Bar at the UAE
The Enterprise Centre
Norwich NR47TJ
Telephone: 01603 630077 /
07540869735
Website: www.mustardcoffeebar.co.uk
With two cafes, the original in one of the oldest and the latest in one of the greenest buildings in Norwich, unique coffee roasted on site and the best in healthy, homemade food.

No 10 Restaurant Sheringham
10 Augusta Street
Sheringham
NR 26 8LA
Telephone: 01263 824400
Website: www.no10Sheringham.co.uk
Family-run restaurant specialising in a 'slow food' approach utilising the very best local produce from Norfolk's north coast to offer a relaxed, intimate dining experience.

Norfolk Food & Drink Limited
c/o Stevenson Consulting
8 Thorpe Road
Norwich
Norfolk NR1 1RY
Telephone: 01603 403660
Website:
www.norfolkfoodanddrink.com
Email:
anna@stevensonconsulting.co.uk
Norfolk Food & Drink is a not for profit organisation which is dedicated to celebrating the burgeoning food and drink industry of Norfolk.

Norfolk Quail Ltd
Highfield Farm
Great Ryburgh
Fakenham
Norfolk NR21 7AL
Telephone: 01328 829249
Website: www.norfolkquail.co.uk
Norfolk Quail is a family business; we are dedicated to the welfare of all our poultry, the wellbeing of our staff, and the satisfaction of our customers.

Norfolk Saffron
21 Norton Street
Burnham Norton
King's Lynn
Norfolk PE31 8DR
Telephone: 07789 366560
Website: www.norfolksaffron.co.uk
We grow award-winning, world-class saffron within sight and sound of the sea, and make wonderful unique products from it: King Harry orange & saffron liqueur, smoked saffron, and saffron flour.

The Norfolk Sloe Company
19 Highfield Road
Fakenham
Norfolk NR21 9DQ
Telephone: 07867 817618
Website:
www.thenorfolksloecompany.com
We are a family business which delights in producing the highest quality premium gin, fruit liqueurs and chocolate truffles by making the most of locally sourced ingredients.

Ollands Farm Foods
Ollands Farm
Short Lane
Happisburgh
Norfolk NR12 0RR
Telephone: 01692 652280
Website:
www.ollands-farm-foods.co.uk
We make a wide range of high quality, award-winning, artisan preserves including marmalades, jams, chutneys, pickles and condiments, sourced locally where possible and handmade with love.

Recruiting Sergeant
Norwich Road
Horstead
Norfolk NR12 7EE
Telephone: 01603 737077
Website: www.recruitingsergeant.co.uk
Award-winning pub and restaurant with rooms known for its food quality, friendliness and attention to detail.

Roger Hickman's
79 Upper St. Giles Street
Norwich
Norfolk NR2 1AB
Telephone: 01603 633522
Website:
www.rogerhickmansrestaurant.com
A fine dining establishment serving modern British food.

Rooftop Gardens
Union Building
51-59 Rose Lane
Norwich
Norfolk NR1 1BY
Telephone: 01603 733044
Website: www.rooftopgardens.co.uk
Dine on the Norwich Skyline: a unique urban venue invites you to eat from our luscious menu, grab a drink from our vibrant bar and enjoy the stunning 360 degree panoramic views.

Samuel's Farm Shop
Market Lane
Walpole
St Andrew
Wisbech
PE14 7LT
Telephone: 01945 781154
Website: www.samuelsfarmshop.co.uk
Samuel's Farm Shop prides itself on providing locally-sourced food at local prices.

Scrummy Pig
Wroxham Barns
Tunstead Rd, Hoveton
Norfolk NR12 8QY
Telephone: 01603 783211
Website: www.scrummypig.co.uk
Produce shop packed with Norfolk Food & Drink based at Wroxham Barns.

Season's Bounty
Unit 1 Loddon Business Centre
2B High Street
Loddon, Norwich
Norfolk NR14 6AH
Telephone: 07796 678490
Website: www.seasons-bounty.co.uk
Maker of multi-awarding winning marmalade and jam.

Shuck's
Drove Orchards
Thornham Road
Thornham, King's Lynn
Norfolk PE36 6LS
Telephone: 01485 525889
Website: www.shucksattheyurt.co.uk
A unique family-run restaurant serving rustic food with a twist from award-winning chef Philip Milner.

Stoke Mill
Mill Road
Stoke Holy Cross
Norwich NR14 8PA
Telephone: 01508 493337
Website: www.stokemill.co.uk
Award-winning food in a beautiful mill at the heart of Norfolk.

Thornage Hall
Thornage
Holt
Norfolk NR25 7QH
Telephone: 01263 860305
Website: www.thornagehall.co.uk
Thornage Hall provides supported living, work and learning opportunities for adults with learning disabilities.

Titchwell Manor Hotel
Titchwell
Norfolk PE31 8BB
Telephone: 01485 472027
Website: www.titchwellmanor.com
A stone's throw from the stunning north Norfolk coast, Titchwell Manor is a beautiful, boutique 27-bedroom country retreat offering destination fine dining.

Walsingham Farms Shop
Guild Street
Little Walsingham
Norfolk NR22 6BU

Walsingham Farms Shop
Caley Mill
Norfolk Lavender
Heacham
Norfolk PE31 7JE
Office: 01328 821888
Walsingham: 01328 821877
Heacham: 01485 570002
Website: www.walsingham.co
Modern and locally focused farm shop. With a butchery, deli, larder, fresh fruit and vegetables.

Wells Crab House Seafood Restaurant
38-40 Freeman Street
Wells-next-the-Sea
Norfolk NR23 1BA
Telephone: 01328 710456
Website: www.wellscrabhouse.co.uk
Wells Crab House offers a dining experience centred around beautifully prepared local and seasonal seafood dishes on the beautiful north Norfolk coast.

The White Horse
4 High Street
Blakeney
Norfolk
NR25 7AL
Telephone: 01263 740574
Website: www.adnams.co.uk/hotels/the-white-horse
Very close to Blakeney Quay on the beautiful north Norfolk coast, The White Horse is a cosy and welcoming pub with characterful accommodation.

Woodforde's Brewery
Slad lane
Woodbastwick
Norfolk NR13 6SW
Telephone: 01603 72033
Website: www.woodfordes.co.uk
Award-winning cask ale brewery in Norfolk.

The INDEX

Other titles in the 'Get Stuck In' series

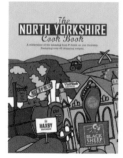

The North Yorkshire Cook Book
features Andrew Pern, Visit York, Made in Malton, Black Sheep Brewery and lots more.
978-1-910863-12-1

The Birmingham Cook Book
features Glynn Purnell, The Smoke Haus, Loaf Bakery, Simpsons and lots more.
978-1-910863-10-7

The Bristol Cook Book
features Dean Edwards, Lido, Clifton Sausage, The Ox, and wines from Corks of Cotham plus lots more.
978-1-910863-14-5

The Oxfordshire Cook Book
features Mike North of The Nut Tree Inn, Sudbury House, Jacobs Inn, The Muddy Duck and lots more.
978-1-910863-08-4

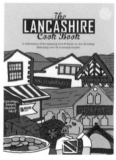

The Lancashire Cook Book
features Andrew Nutter of Nutters Restaurant, Bertram's, The Blue Mallard and lots more.
978-1-910863-09-1

The Liverpool Cook Book
features Burnt Truffle, The Art School, Fraiche, Villaggio Cucina and many more.
978-1-910863-15-2

The Sheffield Cook Book - Second Helpings
features Jameson's Tea Rooms, Craft & Dough, The Wortley Arms, The Holt, Grind Café and lots more.
978-1-910863-16-9

The Leeds Cook Book
features The Boxtree, Crafthouse, Stockdales of Yorkshire and lots more.
978-1-910863-18-3

The Cotswolds Cook Book
features David Everitt-Matthias of Champignon Sauvage, Prithvi, Chef's Dozen and lots more.
978-0-9928981-9-9

The Suffolk Cook Book
features Jimmy Doherty of Jimmy's Farm, Gressingham Duck and lots more.
978-1-910863-02-2

The Manchester Cook Book
features Aiden Byrne, Simon Rogan, Harvey Nichols and lots more.
978-1-910863-01-5

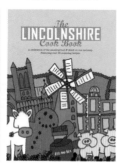

The Lincolnshire Cook Book
features Colin McGurran of Winteringham Fields, TV chef Rachel Green, San Pietro and lots more.
978-1-910863-05-3

The Newcastle Cook Book
features David Coulson of Peace & Loaf, Bealim House, Grainger Market, Quilliam Brothers and lots more.
978-1-910863-04-6

The Cheshire Cook Book
features Simon Radley of The Chester Grosvenor, The Chef's Table, Great North Pie Co., Harthill Cookery School and lots more.
978-1-910863-07-7

The Leicestershire & Rutland Cook Book features Tim Hart of Hambleton Hall, John's House, Farndon Fields, Leicester Market, Walter Smith and lots more.
978-0-9928981-8-2

All books in this series are available from Waterstones, Amazon and independent bookshops.

FIND OUT MORE ABOUT US AT WWW.MEZEPUBLISHING.CO.UK